Claire Smedley currently lives in Thail[illegible] husband after embarking on a nomadic lifestyle mid-pandemic. Selli[illegible] almost everything they owned, they set off on an adventure and freed themselves from physical ties. They reached Thailand, fell in love with it and haven't left. She has one grown-up son, now living the dream as a ski instructor in Switzerland.

Claire has always been fascinated by what it is to be human, a healthy human—in body, mind and spirit. Following a love of science, she got her degrees in biochemistry and chemistry and then began to explore Eastern concepts of health, spirituality and well-being.

Claire was a senior yoga teacher and trainer for almost twenty years and has taught subconscious experiencing for about seven years. She has always had a passion for the less taught aspects of yoga philosophy and breathwork and in 2022 qualified as a Pause Breathwork facilitator—a transformational form of breathwork that helps individuals feel safe and fully present with the whole spectrum of their emotions, traumas, and old wounds.

Following her own self-directed recovery from Hashimoto's Thyroiditis, an autoimmune disease, and lifelong irritable bowel syndrome, she pivoted for a few years to help other women who felt frustrated and disempowered by their autoimmune diseases. She is a qualified Integrative Nutrition Health Coach, with specialisms in gut health and the Autoimmune Paleo Approach (AIP). This period of her life gave rise to her first book, *Nutrition-New Story-New You: Cookbook-Delicious Recipes and Your Guide to Avoiding the Common Pitfalls of the AIP Diet*, which she co-authored with Sue Persad-Patel.

Her work as a health coach brought her full circle back to the kosha model and the perspective that you cannot have great health by only focussing on the body, and that led directly to the desire to write this book.

Claire blends nutrition, yoga, meditation, self-enquiry, subconscious experiencing and breathwork to help people fulfil their potential in life. She works from the premise that there can be no physical health without emotional, mental, and spiritual health, aligned with an intrinsic sense of purpose, unique to each individual.

Claire remains first and foremost a student of life; a teacher second. She is her first and most important client and is committed to walking the inner path so she can help others from experience rather than theory.

For more information on working with Claire, you can email her at *clairesmedleyhealth@gmail.com.*

I dedicate this book to my mum and dad.

Thank you for all the positive programmes you gave me in my early years.

And to my son, Finian, in apology for the programmes I unwittingly gave to you.

Claire Smedley

Living from the Inside Out

Austin Macauley Publishers™
London * Cambridge * New York * Sharjah

A CIP catalogue record for this title is available from the British Library.

ISBN 9781035852949 (Paperback)
ISBN 9781035852956 (ePub e-book)

www.austinmacauley.com

First Published 2024
Austin Macauley Publishers Ltd®
1 Canada Square
Canary Wharf
London
E14 5AA

Gratitude

I have been blessed with so many wonderful teachers and mentors over the years who have encouraged my natural curiosity to learn, especially about the human condition and what it means to live a full and authentic life.

There are too many to mention them all, but in terms of understanding and embodying the material in this book I must give my heartfelt gratitude to Prof William K Mahony, author of *Exquisite Love* and *The Artful Universe*, who was always so empowering. He taught me to trust in my own ideas and interpretations; that my experience with a text or a teaching was valid and just as valid as any scholar. He was always so very clear in this assertion, and it gave me the confidence to own my unique perspectives.

I am also grateful to Prof Douglas Brookes for his unique storytelling abilities and the way he could bring to life and make utterly relevant old stories from centuries ago. He taught me that we are each unique and must receive ourselves as a gift from the universe, that I am the point the universe was trying to make and to stop trying to be like someone else. It took almost twenty years to begin to really embody this truth, but it has been worth the bumpy ride.

More recent mentors include Sylvia Kornas who introduced me to the work of Bob Proctor, delivered with her own unique flair; and she led me to Caroline Caffrey—the Inner Healing Mentor—who guided me through the deep, nitty-gritty work of actually excavating my old wounds, rather than just being aware of them. I am beyond grateful to you, Caroline, for your encouragement to get this book written.

Gratitude also goes out to Samantha Skelly, founder of 'Pause'—the phenomenal breathwork method that has moved me in more ways than I can describe in this book. To Meghan Sandve, my breathwork mentor as I trained as a facilitator in the Pause method who continues to hold the space of transformation for me so skilfully on a regular basis—you're amazing!

I have always been an avid reader and I want to acknowledge all the writers whose works I have enjoyed over the decades—you awakened, fed and directed my path of learning and unknowingly gave me the courage to try to put pen to paper. I have always wanted to write but didn't think I had anything to say, thanks to my limiting beliefs. In reading all your creations, I changed the way I thought about myself: '*If you could do it…then why not I?*'

Thank you, Trevor McGaw, for doing such a thorough and comprehensive job proof-reading the first draft and for your generous support and encouragement.

Huge thanks go to my dear friend and writing collaborator, Sue Persad-Patel, for taking my amateur diagrams and turning them into something far more grown up – love you, my friend.

My thanks also go to everyone at Austin Macauley Publishers for your support in helping me get this book out there, and most especially for taking a leap of faith with a new and unknown author. Thank you.

Finally, but by no means least, thank you to my husband, Neil Smedley, for not only reading, re-reading and proof-reading the draft many times, but for your encouragement, love and support. Thank you for believing in me. Thank you for putting up with months of my procrastination and tolerating my being locked in a room for hours on end.

Table of Contents

It's not simple to say
Most days I don't recognise me
These shoes and this apron
That place and it's patrons
Have taken more than I gave 'em
It's not easy to know
I'm not anything like I used to be
Although it's true
I was never attention sweet centre
I still remember that girl
She's imperfect but she tries
She is good but she lies
She is hard on herself
She is broken and won't ask for help
She is messy but she's kind
She is lonely most of the time
She is all of this mixed up
And baked in a beautiful pie
She is gone but she used to be mine
It's not what I asked for
Sometimes life just slips in through a back door
And carves out a person
And makes you believe it's all true
And now I've got you
And you're not what I asked for
If I'm honest I know I would give it all back
For a chance to start over
And rewrite an ending or two
For the girl that I knew

Who'd be reckless just enough
Who can hurt but
Who learns how to toughen up when she's bruised
And gets used by a man who can't love
And then she'll get stuck and be scared
Of the life that's inside her
Growing stronger each day
'Til it finally reminds her
To fight just a little
To bring back the fire in her eyes
That's been gone but it used to be mine
She is messy but she's kind
She is lonely most of the time
She is all of this mixed up
And baked in a beautiful pie
She is gone but she used to be mine

She Used to be Mine
What's Inside: Songs from Waitress
~ Sarah Bareilles

Introduction

Do you ever feel as if life is a bit like trying to do a jigsaw puzzle without the box? You have all the pieces or most of them, but without the picture to guide you, putting it all together feels impossible. You try and try and get nothing but frustration for all your struggling hard work.

This was how I felt for so many years, and when I was diagnosed with a chronic illness three years ago and told there wasn't anything I could do except take medications. I knew I had to get serious about pulling my life-pieces together. I knew I had all the pieces, after all, I had two science degrees, I had been studying and teaching yoga for twenty years, meditating for ten, learning about natural remedies for five and thought I knew how to look after myself…and yet I still got sick.

The majority of chronic illnesses come from slow erosion caused by something harmful done repeatedly. Essentially, it's usually (not always, but *usually*) the result of your habits—habits of doing and habits of thinking.

On the surface, I appeared to be doing everything right, so what was I missing?

I kept looking, kept thinking that the next new thing would be the missing piece, but I sensed that I already had all the pieces—I needed to see how to put them all together, stop looking for answers outside of myself and, truly get back into my body and the infinite wisdom that was available there.

I soon realised that in my search for health and a successful career, I had become trapped in my head but disconnected from my body. My body and my life were things I had to manage, fix and control. As a result, I was ignoring what my body was trying to show me—that I was living a life which was out of alignment with my heart…or what you might also call my soul…my true self, and who I was here to be.

In a moment of uncomfortable, humbling honesty with myself, I admitted that much of my 'spiritual practice' had been performative self-care: I was going through the motions, ticking it off my to-do list and giving myself a pat on the back…but not really going beneath the surface for long enough to really feel my own emotional pain.

It was during my first powerful, activating breathwork session that I accessed something deeper inside. I cried in that session for the first time in years. I found my emotions again, maybe even for the first time, and then something remarkable happened—my frozen shoulder, which had been rigid for ten months, started to become free…coincidence? No, I don't think so.

As my emotions and my body started to loosen, and the need to control every aspect of my life abated, I began to tap back into my intuition again. It was a lot like relearning a language you haven't spoken for years, but it slowly started to come back again. I began to understand it; tentatively trust it, and it felt like home.

Then one day, prompted by my intuition, I remembered an ancient map of the human being from my yoga studies, and realised that I had in fact possessed the box all along! Now, armed with this map, I could start putting all the pieces together, with the same sense of peaceful joy that I get from doing real jigsaw puzzles.

The roadmap is a model from around 2,600 years ago, from an ancient Indian text called *The Taittiriya Upanishad* and it is very simple to understand (easier than pronouncing it). Healing doesn't have to be complex, in fact, it rarely is. We already have too much complexity in our lives, getting back to simplicity is a return to our natural state. Simplicity includes stillness, space, and silence—three of life's greatest healers which allow us to access presence and permission.

That's when I knew I had to write this book. The map might be ancient, but it is more relevant today than ever before, as we find ourselves in a world with so much low-grade unwellness, stress and depression, right up to epidemic levels of anxiety and chronic illness. We were not supposed to spend our lives feeling this broken! We are here to thrive! I read recently that one in eight people in the UK are currently on the NHS waiting list for treatment—this level of disease is crazy! You don't need a PhD in science to live a healthy and fulfilling life. Everyone can access it because it's your inheritance.

If you have a sense that your life is supposed to be more than it is, then this book is for you. If you struggle with persistent physical or mental ill health, lack of joy and purpose, or feel disconnected from who you really are, then I hope, through this book, to give you a simple map, with actionable steps so you can begin to build that wonderful life you sense inside which is currently eluding you. It's time to bring it out and start living it by following the wisdom within your body, a wisdom older than time. Grab a pen, this book is going to be interactive, full permission to write all over the pages!

What this book is not:

My intention with this offering is not to create a scholarly interpretation of this old text. There are people far, far more qualified than me to do that and I am not interested in sharing a precise and detailed translation. I don't want to put more stuff in your head…we are already living far too much in our head, with more and more information bombarding us, each and every day.

What this book is hoping to be:

I hope to keep to the spirit of the original teaching and make it a very practical guide to help you live a more fulfilling and vibrant life, connected to both your source energy and fully and joyfully participating in the world around you—your life! It's a book to be contemplated, digested, and implemented over time. The map holds up a mirror so you can see where you might be unknowingly working against your own best interests. The teachings are designed to be integrated into your life slowly, step by step. By referring back to this book often, I hope you come to treat it as your handbook to happiness.

We are each born free, free to craft a life based on the particular blueprint within us. Just as every acorn knows how to become an oak tree and contains all the guidance it needs within itself, so you too were born to become the amazing, unique and wonderful human being that you are. You already have all that you need to become that version of yourself and experience delight in the process. Delight is perhaps the most important ingredient of your life.

This is your birth right, and the birth right of every one of us on the planet—no exceptions! There is no one exactly like you and there never has been—you are unique, and you are brilliant just as you are.

So where did we go wrong?

Our sense of who we are got blurred along the way to the point that we may have lost all connection with it. We started living a protective life based on what we 'should' do, and who the world and its distorted norms told us we 'should' be. We compromised our uniqueness for something far more mundane—we tried to be somebody else to fit in, and we started believing the lies in our heads.

Bruce Lipton, PhD, in his wonderful work *The Biology of Belief*, reminds us that a cell can either protect itself or grow, but it can't do both at the same time. You, as a colony of cells, can also only do one at a time. So, all the time you live in a state of protection, trying to be someone acceptable to others, you cannot grow, expand, and fully experience your own true potential. It's as if you're putting the brakes on ever truly becoming that magnificent oak tree that you came here to be.

I often felt that I would like to return to the factory setting I was born with, so that I could start all over again, but this time I would be the one programming me, not other people. We do this each time we buy a new computer, and we can do it for ourselves too.

This doesn't mean to imply there is a quick fix—it's going to take all the patience you would bring to a 5000-piece jigsaw puzzle, but it doesn't have to be joyless. In fact, if the process of unbecoming all that you are not, and becoming who you are, isn't revealing more and more joy in your life, then I would say you are doing it all wrong. There will be times when it all feels sticky, difficult, and uncomfortable, and you'll want to give up. But change is not as uncomfortable as staying where you are…stuck in a life that you know doesn't fit you.

What follows is my take on this ancient map—the Five Koshas—the five layers of you, the contents of which either allow you to live your life—one of expansion, joy, love, meaning, freedom and wonder, or the contents stand in the way of that life, instead creating a life of mediocrity and dissatisfaction.

Each kosha is a gateway to a greater understanding of what you have accumulated through life, the depository of your past and how the past might still be getting in the way of the life you are trying to live today. All five koshas play out in the physical body, so getting back into your body, really feeling it, going deep below the surface and into the sensations within it, and fiercely loving it, is how you start reclaiming, healing, and integrating all the parts of yourself.

Remember that this model is over 2,600 years old. Recent scientific research is revealing more about how exactly the body and mind are connected and interwoven. There is no doubt now that, not only do the mind and body communicate with each other, they are *within* each other, they are one. I love it when science finally catches up with ancient wisdom traditions. One day I see a time when there is no conflict at all between science and spirituality, after all, they are both trying to map and explain the mysteries of this life. Spirituality approaches life from within; science from the outside in and at some point, they intermingle and inform one another.

No doctor can address all your layers. No pill can address all your layers. But you can, and *only* you can, because only you know what it *feels* like to be inside your body and those feelings will guide you back to health and well-being if you let them. It's not complex—you have the capacity to do this. There is no greater life's work than becoming gloriously and unapologetically you.

Perhaps you picked up this book because, like me, you have a health condition you want to heal. Or maybe because you have reached mid-life when, so often, you get prompted to review your life at the halfway point and ask yourself if the next half is going to be more of the same, a steady decline or something better. Or maybe you just have an underlying, nagging sense that there is more on offer for you, but you can't quite seem to access it.

It doesn't matter the motivation behind picking up this book—you did! Go with that! You are a unique human being put on this earth to live your unique, joyful, and creative life. The Kosha Map was designed to support every one of us. One map, applied in an infinite number of ways. Use this book to unlock your true self, release all the stuff that doesn't allow that true self to come through and start to build a life you love.

I am excited that you are here. Let's dive in!

Part 1
Who You Really Are

Chapter 1
Your Birth

Cast your mind back to the day that you were born. Of course, you have no retrievable memory of that moment, any 'memories' you have are physical imprints of the event and the stories and memories of others—the people who were present at the time. You have a second-hand memory at best, filled with all the personal biases of the storytellers.

Maybe it was a long, difficult labour. In which case, your mother's story may be full of pain, fear, and then overwhelming joy—quite a combination! Perhaps your father felt unable to help and that left him feeling vulnerable and impotent—his story will be full of these emotions. As for the medical professional who delivered you…well, the memory of your birth may have been forgotten altogether, lost in a filing cabinet of hundreds of similar births.

So, what is the 'truth'? Well, it depends. We tend to think of the truth as a concrete, actual thing, but in reality, we live in a world of relationships and stories. We make our own meaning and so truth changes. A better question becomes: in this moment, what is *real* for me, what is present?

You arrived—that's a truth and the only truth that matters. You stepped into a life, into a body and into your own story, one which you were free to write for yourself but in the early years, most of your story was written by others. It doesn't have to stay that way. You are free to grab the quill, turn over a blank page and start over.

When you arrived, you were equipped with everything you needed to live your unique life to its fullest potential, a life no one else ever gets to experience. Other people may have judged you imperfect according to their ideals, but their ideals have nothing to do with you. Maybe your father wanted a son and instead, you arrived as a daughter…to him, you might have been a disappointment.

It hurts, which is a real feeling in the body, but it's not true! You are not a disappointment, you're a miracle! You contained everything you needed to be fully you. However, growing up in an environment where you instinctively and energetically 'knew' you weren't good enough, even before you could understand what was going on, would have been enough to shape you with a belief that you needed to prove yourself worthy of love and worthy of existence.

But I am jumping ahead.

Let's go back to the day you were born before any stories were told. You arrived full of yourself. Literally, full to the skin and beyond, of the essence of you, pure awareness and with a life force pulsing through you, infinitely creative and full of possibilities. It's funny when you start paying attention to language, how many 'truths' have been distorted into criticisms. Has anyone ever said to you, "Oh, you're so full of yourself"? Trust me, it's not used as a compliment, but it should be…oh, to be so uninhibited! The underlying message though is, "Don't be yourself, don't be wonderful, don't be free, you have to dumb down and fit in, be like everyone else." So, we enter into a collective agreement, that we will strive to be like everyone else and not shine, and so begins the descent into mediocrity and dissatisfaction.

You arrived full of yourself—in a good way. You had a soul with bespoke gifts. You were aware of yourself and the world around you. You had life energy coursing through you like electricity, and you had an amazing brand-new vehicle called a human body. You had no idea how to drive it yet, but it was fun to explore. You didn't feel separate from the power of life but an intimate part of it. You were not afraid of the unknown back then, because *everything* was unknown. There was no 'outside your comfort zone' to be afraid of because there was no comfort zone yet; there was no fear.

In the beginning, you experienced and expressed abundance and expansion—unobstructed, outward-flowing energy. If you were hungry, you freely expressed that; if you wanted something, you reached out for it. Every waking moment was infused with wonder, curiosity, creativity and joy, and you loved it.

The automatic part of your nervous system (called the autonomic nervous system) ran all the essential functions so you didn't need to get involved: your heart was beating without you making it happen; you were breathing; you could extract nutrients from milk; your cells knew how to divide so that you could grow. Your intelligent life force was living through you, as you. How flipping amazing is that! You didn't have to learn any of it—Life simply 'knew' how to function. Oh, except for regulating bowel and bladder function—I still haven't really figured out why that isn't automatic at birth. Perhaps back then it was just that we could easily let go of what we didn't need, effortlessly…whereas now, as an adult letting go is really hard.

Even before you were born you grew by some invisible, creative impulse to be: to become this one-of-a-kind human edition. There is a divine intelligence that just knows how to grow a human being—from one pattern it makes an entirely different human every single time. It knows which of your trillions of genetically identical cells will become bone cells, nerve cells, skin cells, immune cells, and muscle cells. They all look and behave differently but all this diversity arises from one genetic blueprint for you.

One bundle of DNA—your DNA—becomes all the seemingly different cells and functions in your body. How does it know? And why are we not astounded by this? The diversity of life is the most incredible miracle there is, and we are blind to it. But the day you were born, your entire being knew this and you experienced the wonder and delight of it directly. You didn't need to control it or improve it. You didn't have language yet, you needed to learn that. I'm talking about a knowing that is soul-deep, pre-language, a knowing which comes from experience, a knowing which is felt…and to feel, you need a body because that's where feeling plays out.

One of the highest emotions you can experience is wonder, a deep awe-filled curiosity that drives you to explore, to experience more and more things. It's an inquiry into the mystery, the great uncharted territory of life, the future, the unknown. To tap back into curiosity, you first need to be willing to admit that you don't know something. Curiosity is the mother of creativity and your soul longs to express its creative power, and once again, that's where your body comes in.

When was the last time you were really connected to awe-filled curiosity? When were you last curious about something…not something you could Google to get a quick answer, I mean *really* curious, where you were willing to explore and take the time to learn about it in real depth. It's sad to note that many people stop learning when they leave school, curiosity becomes shut down and life becomes repetitive.

That's why so many of us love to travel and experience new cultures, new food and landscapes—it connects us back to that place of not-knowing, of exploration. Exploration of any kind is a form of growth—growth into the unknown spaces around us, and so our knowledge and experiences increase. By default, if you're not exploring, you're protecting.

Other things awaken our dormant sense of wonder and curiosity too—sunsets and sunrises, vast landscapes, and expansive, star-studded night skies. When we connect with awe we are arrested, our mind stops, our breath stops, and in that pause, we are reminded of who we truly are—a part of this mystery; we are reborn into wonder. There is a power in the mystery, in the unknown. Somewhere along the way, we became fearful of it, we tried to know everything because that felt safe, and life…well, that was the trade-off—life, in many ways, became mundane and predictable.

When you arrived, this is who you were! You were fascinated by everything. What does a lemon taste like? Ooh, not nice, so your face automatically puckered, and the memory was lodged to avoid a future 'not nice' experience—those yellow oval things don't taste good. You started to experience, and you began to catalogue those experiences so you could safely pursue what you love and leave what you don't love for someone else.

It should have been that simple. But you were not the only one giving yourself experiences, there was a tribe of others around you too and they started to create entries in that catalogue, as well as all the events of your early life. Even now, in your adult life, you are being programmed by popular culture, social media algorithms, the news, emotionally impactful or traumatic experiences and so on.

As a baby, in your factory settings, you were having the most amazing time learning how to drive this vehicle called your body, spontaneously exploring and experiencing the fascinating world around you. It's worth making the point here that just because you puckered your face in response to a lemon, that it wasn't a 'bad' experience. Those labels came much later when we began to learn a language and interact with other people and more importantly, their opinions. As a baby, you simply expressed your preferences. A lemon is a lemon (and a perfect addition to a gin and tonic) and it is neither good nor bad—it just is.

As a baby, you responded to your preferences—lemons are not for me, you didn't blame the lemon or feel any need to change it or destroy it. You simply left it alone and went back to exploring and having fun.

Your deepest truth is that you are a soul who came here to create and express life according to what lights *you* up and to pursue whatever you are drawn to pursue. You never stopped being a soul, full of delight, wonder and free expression, but you might have lost contact with that part of yourself somewhere along the way as you began to prioritise safety over curiosity; predictability over surprise; and other people's desires over your own.

Take a moment and really allow the miracle of your own existence to soak in. One creative intelligence becomes many souls, just as one ocean can become an infinite number of drops of water. One cell becomes all the different structures within your body. You learned how to live in and use this body to navigate the world because of an inherent desire and curiosity to experience all that life had on offer for you.

Do you really think a mistake was made? That for some reason, joy, love and freedom of expression were denied you? Is that just for other people?

No! Remember there is one blueprint which makes all humans, just like there is one blueprint that makes all oak trees. Each acorn contains all it needs to fully evolve into a magnificent oak tree. Each oak tree is distinct and different from all other oaks, but they are all pure expressions of an oak and life unfolding beautifully and continuously. Do you think an oak tree feels doubt? Does she compare herself with other oak trees and feel that she's not good enough? Of course not. Do you think that same oak tree wants to fight and argue with another oak tree because it's growing in a different way?

Nature and divine intelligence didn't 'miss you out'—your body may not look like someone else's—so what? It's time to stop comparing yourself with everyone else because they are not you. Reclaim the miracle that you are.

One of my dearest teachers comes to mind here. Professor Bill Mahony would talk about the material world we live in and the vast unfathomable size of the universe, and with a beaming smile and eyes alight with wonder, would say, "It so easily could have been nothing at all and yet here we all are!" His eyes would sparkle like a child's and his wonder was magnetic, drawing us all into the sheer awesomeness of life.

It's time to lovingly receive the part of yourself that you fully embraced as a baby but have become estranged from as you started to grow—she never went away, she's still inside you…waiting to play. The invitation throughout this book is to excavate your soul, your heart, your true self—it doesn't matter what you name it, because she's something you feel rather than describe; any attempt to put her into words always feels somewhat inadequate. Piece by piece, let go of everything that blocks you from her and live from the inside out.

Imagine a world where everyone was accepted as their own, uninhibited, and radiant soul…including you. Soak into how you would feel in that world, as that uninhibited version of you, then multiply that by eight billion souls…wow, what a world that would be! An eight-billion-piece jigsaw puzzle, coming together to reveal one beautiful picture of unity. A unity *because* of our differences, not because we have all become identical on the outside.

Until you do live as your full, factory-setting self, you will never be free, you will never feel at ease, you will always sway to the opinions and expectations of others in your world, and you will suffer—emotionally, mentally, physically, and spiritually. It's time to be you, to feel worthy, loveable, special, free and to live in abundant energy, joy, and love. You get to give all this back to yourself. No one else can give you to yourself. You must choose to claim her.

Chapter 2
How You Got Dented

So, if you arrived curious, wide open and full of your sense of self…what happened? Why did you stop feeling like that?

Just like a blank, brand-new computer, you became shaped and programmed by your environment. This included your family home, community and community groups, school, the programming received by all the people in these groups and the collective culture and beliefs of society, going back generations. Basically, the whole world started to tell you how you should be, and you started to censor yourself to fit in and chances are, you've been doing it ever since. This need to be accepted is a strong impulse in all of us because we are tribal people, wired for connection. Being unacceptable risks being rejected, kicked out of the tribe, and left as food for the lions. This need for acceptance runs deep and can be found behind most of our self-limiting beliefs. In fact, all fear can be traced back to the fear of rejection because historically, that meant imminent death.

Imagine yourself at birth as a bright, hollow, silver ball—expansive, full, and pristine. Something hits you, like being told off or being misunderstood—"Ooh that didn't feel nice," and it left a dent in your sense of self, your silver ball. You got over the immediate energetic and physical shock and got back to playing and exploring. But what if you got hit again, in the same place, the same unhealed wound? It's really going to hurt this time and leave a deeper dent. Now there's a part of you that doesn't feel full and expansive anymore so you found ways to protect it from being hurt again. Remember, you can't grow and protect yourself at the same time, so now there's a part of you that stays small.

At a soul level, you know that hurting others isn't normal behaviour. You start to wonder if maybe there's something wrong with you to attract such pain. Perhaps you need to hide parts of yourself from others in case they find you out to be less than perfect.

In your first ten years, this was happening all the time. You couldn't reason with it because you hadn't developed that skill yet, so you instinctively protected yourself from getting dented again. You developed protective behaviours which served you at that time in your life so you could continue to play and explore…but they became protective habits.

You carried those same protective behaviours into your adult life and as you got older, you created stories and justifications around them…all pure fiction.

Let me give you an example.

Say, you lived in a house where there was a lot of anger expressed. You were busy playing, loving being you, exploring and out of the blue that anger was directed at you. You may not have been able to understand the words being shouted, but you were completely able to feel the energy and the threat to your well-being. Children are masters at picking up energy or 'vibes' from people and environments, just as animals are. If you were unfortunate enough to receive more than angry words, then the physical pain would have created an even bigger wound, a profound dent in your sense of fullness.

If this happened once, it may have had no real lasting impact, and you would expand again, pushing out those dents and kinks from the inside. But if it was a constant undertone of your childhood or a period of it, you would have started to protect yourself instinctively:

- You may have instinctively known when the emotional energy around you was dangerous and moved away from it. Perhaps retreating to your room, a hidden corner somewhere or leaving the house entirely.
- You may have tried to fight it, kicking back at the angry person or even random people.
- You may have become hypervigilant, scanning every environment trying to read the energy of the room and determine where and who felt safe so that you would feel more in control, prepared for any eventuality.
- You may have become an excessive people pleaser, always trying to stay on someone's good side so they wouldn't get angry, so they would love and protect you, essentially trying to manage the emotions of everyone around you.
- You may have become a servant, doing everything you can to create a calm environment, doing the chores, being helpful, being a 'good girl'.
- You may have escaped into fantasy, losing yourself in books, make-believe and imaginary friends so you didn't have to feel the emotional pain.

- Or you may have tried to numb out the painful and confusing feelings you could do nothing about, by watching television, playing video games and later on, turning to substances like food, drugs and alcohol.

It's worth emphasising that none of this was done as a conscious decision. The same autonomic part of your nervous system that knows how to grow your physical body also has a keen sense of survival. This was all automatic, instinctive, and totally normal.

But then, you evolved from instinctive actions to creating stories and fiction to try to make some sort of sense of why all of this was happening, common stories being:

- I am a bad person
- I am not loveable
- I have to do more to be accepted
- If I can just do everything perfectly then I will be safe, acceptable
- I am not worthy
- I am not good enough
- The world is a dangerous place
- Feelings are overwhelming, I am not going there
- Everything is my fault
- I have to defend myself
- No one is going to help me, it's all down to me
- I have to change myself to be acceptable because there is something wrong with me

The trouble is this is *not* something you outgrow; it stays like computer software and you'll be able to see these protective behaviours showing up in your adult life. When someone around you expresses anger, that automatic programming kicks in to protect you just as it did when you were four years old, reacting in the same way you adopted at the age you first needed it to keep you safe. Maybe your default is escape, and you find yourself instantly retreating, shutting down and keeping out of the way, rather than adopting a more appropriate response and asserting your boundaries—letting the other person know they have crossed a line and that it's not okay.

If you truly want to reclaim your lost fullness, you need to release the past, release these outdated protective behaviours, which helped you once but are hindering you now, so you can respond in a genuine and mature way to the *actual* moment you find yourself in. This is true freedom—to be able to authentically respond to life, moment by moment, without the burden of history and narratives from the past getting in the way.

Now, I have chosen an extreme example of anger, and you may be thinking, '*Well, I'm okay because I didn't grow up in an angry house.*' So often, I hear people say, "I had a normal childhood." I've said it myself, and those words reveal a story of their own…for what is normal? It's just something familiar to you. So, in our storytelling minds, we are all living a 'normal' life.

We all got dented, in different ways but there isn't a single person who is still a pristine and shiny silver ball. Everything you think and do, and everything that happens to you and around you, leaves an impression—a smudge of some sort. Some events dent you a little, some dent you like the Grand Canyon. Other events and people in your life help to push the dents out and expand you again, and others deepen the groove of the old wound.

It's important to state here that it isn't a competition. Your dents are not to be compared with anyone else's. It's all too easy to say, *"Well, I can't complain, there are people who have had a much harder time than me."* All this does is give you an excuse not to address your issues, which is a form of self-abandonment. It is none of your business what wounds other people are healing, it is your business to heal your own wounds as you discover them, because as you'll see as we go through the book, your early wounds are still running your life, governing your decisions, affecting your physical and mental health, all of your relationships and everything you do.

It's also worth mentioning there is no value in allocating blame for what has been done to you. Yes, it was unfair and for some people, horrific. It never makes a hurtful behaviour right, but the people who wounded you were wounded too. Lashing out with blame and more hurt towards those people (and innocent bystanders) only contributes to more hurt in the world and more seething resentment in you. The only way to break the cycle of hurt is to make it stop here by healing yourself so that you don't inadvertently hurt yourself or others in your effort to protect yourself in outdated ways.

When I started to learn this and began the lifelong path of healing my broken parts, a lot of guilt arose rather than blame. I could forgive and understand that the things that had dented me had nothing to do with me or my worthiness. It wasn't personal. What I really struggled with was how I had potentially impacted my son when I was raising him from my wounded self. This came from my own deep-seated story that when things go wrong, it is always my fault. I had to learn how to let go of that story, remember that I was doing the best I could with the knowledge I had, and trust that he would find his way to healing his wounds too, and hopefully before he becomes a father himself. It was an uncomfortable healing process, a jagged edge I still rub up against from time to time. Sometimes the healing can feel worse than living with the pain, but it tends to be short-lived rather than lifelong, so I encourage you to persevere through it.

The poet, Philip Larkin, sums it up perfectly:

This Be the Verse

They fuck you up, your mum and dad.
They may not mean to, but they do.
They fill you with the faults they had
And add some extra, just for you.
But they were fucked up in their turn
By fools in old-style hats and coats,
Who half the time were soppy-stern
And half at one another's throats.
Man hands on misery to man.
It deepens like a coastal shelf.
Get out as early as you can,
And don't have any kids yourself.

I don't advocate for such a drastic conclusion as not having children for they are our greatest teachers. They hold up a mirror for us to really start to look at who we show up as in the world. But we can get out of the cycle of passing on our inherited dysfunction. There is room for forgiveness here, of others and of ourselves, so that we can create a life of joy and self-acceptance. Forgiveness is a huge part of the process of coming back to wholeness.

Remember that you are the pure version of yourself that arrived at your birth. You are not your programming, you simply picked that up, much of which was faulty, full of bugs and errors. You wouldn't expect your computer to function at its best with faulty software and computer viruses. So, you clean up your computer, run software updates, and install anti-virus software to keep it clean and running optimally. You can bring the same approach to yourself.

Our koshas, our layers are designed to bring out the best in us—literally. They are designed to automate the outward flow of curiosity, creativity, joy, love, spontaneity, and life force so that our natural state of being is expressed in all that we do.

But our layers have become clogged like dirty air filters—not just from our childhood, but every day, from what we continue to allow in. Oftentimes you are allowing in more fear, more judgement, more intolerance, more comparison, and so on. Our work is to regularly clean out the layers so more of the inner light can come through, and stop putting new junk in. We can choose what we give our time and attention to, what we allow in, how we affirm our boundaries and what we choose to pursue in life.

So, if you are ready for the biggest spring clean of your life, read on.

Chapter 3
An Ancient Model for an Inspired Life

There is an ancient and beautiful map containing everything you need to live an inspired life. The true beauty of this map lies in its simplicity. We live in a ridiculously complex world, and simplicity is the antidote for modern life.

Think about how complicated, busy, and demanding your daily life is as you navigate parenting, your career, transportation, keeping up with household chores, balancing financial pressures, technology (great when it works, but when it doesn't…!) and so on. Your solution might be to escape on holiday, spend long lazy days at the beach and rest. It's interesting how many of us are naturally drawn to simplicity on holidays, such as visiting laid-back fishing villages, the countryside, or camping—a return to a slower, in many ways richer, pace of life. Your soul is craving simplicity, and holidays work in the short term because 'simple and slow' restores your sense of self…and then you go straight back into the chaos or everyday life and start the cycle again. Sound familiar?

Healing is to be found in being less complex. Left alone, the impulse that knows how to grow your body from a single cell also knows how to heal you. The body can heal itself often enough if you just give it the right conditions, none of which are complicated. Most of the time, we just need to step out of the way and stop trying so hard to fix everything.

You know this to be true, but maybe you've forgotten, or you have been conditioned to fix and fight everything your whole life. In which case I invite you to spend two minutes contemplating a scab. Yes, a scab. You get a cut and without any interference from you or anyone else, within a day or two your body has grown a scab to heal the wound and protect the whole of you from infection. You didn't have to think about it or focus on it or learn how to do it by searching the internet. You didn't have to ask ten people for their advice on how best to do it (and get ten different answers). It just happened. Scabs are daily miracles but are easy to dismiss as insignificant. Really, they are humble, yet tangible, demonstrations of how your life force simply knows how to live, to thrive, to bring itself back to balance and heal. We are surrounded by these humble and overlooked daily miracles, we just need to slow down to notice them.

So, let's look at this beautiful, simple map—The Five Koshas Model.

This model of the human being is about 2,600 years old and comes from India, home to some of the most insightful observations of life that are still deeply relevant today.

You can think of a kosha as a layer, a sheathing, a little like the layers of an onion. I sometimes think of them as different, overlapping bodies or aspects of ourselves, or even coats we wear, but for simplicity, let's call them layers.

There are five layers, and from the inside out they are:

1. The joy layer—This is the deep, natural, outward-flowing, and effervescent joy for life. This layer contains the personal aspects that light you up, and the natural impulses to reach out into the world to connect with it.
2. The wisdom layer—This can also be called the subconscious, memory, or habit mind—it's the automatic in your life, and it's also where we access universal wisdom.
3. The thinking layer—Here we find our thoughts and it's where we process all the input from the senses. It's for learning new things from the world around us and making sense of it, making meaning.
4. The energy layer—Also known as the aura or energy field is where you experience emotions and vitality, closely associated with your breathing.
5. The physical layer—Also known as the body of food, this layer is your physical structure and all of your biological functions.

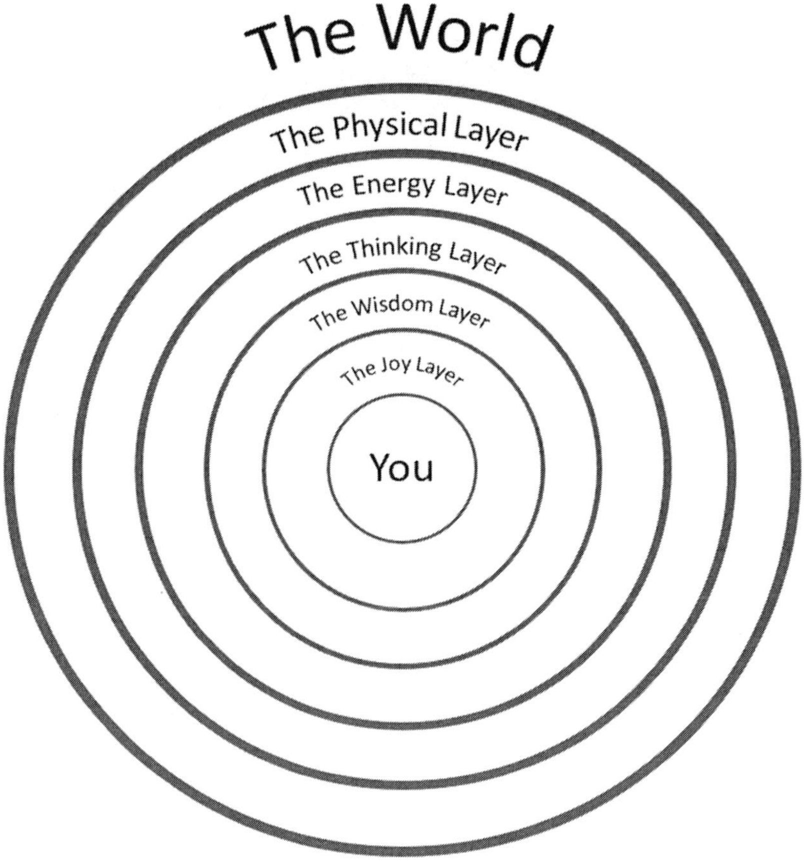

And driving it all is you. None of the layers are really you, they are the vehicle you inhabit, and get to experience life through. You are at the centre, you are the pure, creative life force animating it all, with your hands on the steering wheel, directing the vehicle.

You are the same stuff as the universe itself. You are the same awe-inspiring intelligence that was able to grow your body from a single cell. You are not separate from it, but you think you are because you identify yourself as the layers, the vehicle rather than the driver.

If you have seen films on virtual reality, such as Avatar, where a person enters a pod and suddenly, they are controlling a different body and having an alternative experience of reality, then you have a pretty good analogy for what is actually happening right now—only the body and mind you are driving is the e you are in. You live through it, but you are not it. You create your life but even your life is not who you are, it's what you created.

Don't like your life? Create a new one. Only your mind and your old stories think it's impossible, that you're stuck with this life. You are reacting to life around you, essentially living life from the outside in, believing the story that the world is fixed and out of your control. This goes against your very design. You are a creator of life, not a reactor to it. You are meant to live from the inside out. You have come to believe the stories in your mind as true, but they're not.

In the following chapters, we'll go deeper into what distorts each of your layers and how you can cleanse and heal them, but first let's have a quick overview of what they are and what they govern. Let's cover some basic attributes and symptoms of disease in each layer. We'll look at them in reverse order, starting with the more tangible, which might be easier to relate to:

The Physical Layer

This layer is 'the body of food'. It is constructed from the raw materials you consume as food and drink, but also drugs and other toxic, unnatural substances. Your cells are replacing themselves constantly and apart from a few cells that you have had since birth, no cell or structure in your body is more than seven years old! Even your bones. You are recreating yourself all the time in accordance with the pattern held in your deeper layers. It will stay on the same path, regenerating you exactly the same, over and over until you decide that you want to create yourself differently.

As well as food, the body belongs to the wider biological world and needs certain things to thrive: proper hydration, rest and sleep, to be in alignment with the light-dark cycle of day and night, movement, and to be free from poisons and toxins.

Symptoms in the body are the most obvious and tangible. They show up as pain, dysfunction, digestive problems, immune problems, headaches, rashes, acute and chronic illnesses, and so on. They can arise from within the physical kosha itself—because you are not attending to your biological needs—nutrients, fuel, sleep and movement, etc., or from one of the deeper layers, such as from your thoughts, beliefs and emotions all playing out in the body. For example, the fact that you choose not to nourish the physical body properly can come from a deeper-held belief that you are not worthy of it, or it's too difficult: stories, even unconscious ones, determine choices.

The Energy Layer

We are energetic, animated and vibrant beings, distinctly different from rocks. We get our energy from many sources not just food, but also from the air, sunlight, the earth, other people, passions and tapping into the wider energetic web from which we came, and to which we are always connected, what we might call 'source energy'.

Energy is circulated through the body in several different ways and at several different rates, depending on how that energy is going to be used. Not unlike the different amperages in your various household appliances—your oven runs on a higher rate of energy flow than a light bulb because they serve different purposes.

Breath and emotions come to life in this layer too. These are two of your most powerful flows of energy and information and that's the key attribute of this layer: whilst the physical body is about structure and mechanics, the energy body is about vibration, flow, and interconnection—both within the body and with the outside world.

Symptoms of disease here include fatigue, emotional overwhelm, emotional shutdown, breathing problems, circulatory problems, rigidity of body and mind, stagnant energy, fear, anxiety and excess energy, as well as depression and energy depletion.

The Thinking (Conscious) Mind Layer

This is where many people live out their lives, especially these days thanks to having constant access to the internet in their hands. Cut off from the body and the soul, they neglect the needs of both. Instead, they try really hard to figure everything out, control all variables, strive for perfection and a predictable, safe life based on what worked in the past. These are all symptoms of disease at this level. Other symptoms might show up as being indecisive, unable to reason, being stuck in one point of view, lacking imagination or creativity.

Dis-ease in this layer is also found in people with busy minds which they can't seem to switch off, who are unable to focus or concentrate and have a really hard time meditating. The content of this layer is often repetitive and junk thoughts, playing in a loop.

Too many people are trying to control their lives with their minds, thinking about what to do with their lives rather than just living in flow from moment to moment. Control is not what this part of the mind is for. It's for learning new things so you can continue to pursue what you love, more easily.

The Habit (Automatic or Subconscious) Mind Layer

This part of you is supposed to be about making as much of your daily life as automatic as possible—it works so that you can play. It also wants to keep you alive so that you can live your wonderful life for as long as possible. However, all too often it has been programmed by other people in ways that limit you, hold you back, or cause you to fall back into patterns of self-sabotage. Obsessed with safety and protection, life starts to feel like a prison because your soul wants to explore, expand, and experience new things. After all, a boat is safe in the harbour, but to sit in a harbour isn't why a boat was created.

Have you ever been caught between wanting to do something (from your soul) and yet finding yourself doing the exact opposite? Such as wanting to lose weight but then succumbing to a large slice of cake—you know you want to lose weight because you feel more alive when you do, but you eat the cake anyway. This is your subconscious mind at play because it drives 95% of what you do, and you are mostly oblivious to it because, by definition, it's not conscious, it is automatic.

Some of the content of this layer you were born with. It was pre-programmed—such as how to digest food, fight infections, grow scabs, breathe, beat your heart, fall asleep and wake up again and so on. The rest has been learned—something learned through repetition until it became automatic—a habit. Everything from how to walk or tie your shoelaces, to how you feel about yourself, your worth, your place in the world, and what you deserve. That collection of habits and beliefs creates your sense of identity: your self-image or ego. However, your sense of identity is not you, it's something you have accumulated.

Disease here shows up in your behaviours and actions, your beliefs and your self-talk.

The Joy Layer

This is the delight of being alive. This layer teaches us that existing is wonderful, literally—full of wonder and something to revel in. Symptoms of disease here can be a feeling of joylessness, hopelessness, flatness, no sense of purpose, life is nothing but suffering and despondency. These symptoms invariably come from the outer layers which have become so thick with their own content and symptoms that the joy just cannot flow through them and be experienced. You forget that joy is there, you deny it, you buy into the collective belief that fun is for children and now you're an adult, life is going to be a struggle, just get on with it. Is that a belief you want to keep? If not, you can change it.

There are some basic ideas to keep in mind when working with the koshas:

1. You, as the driver of this magnificent vehicle, sit at the centre of it all. Your sense of yourself, your soul, flows from this centre, through all the layers. You experience your soul, the miracle of your own life in every layer—the mind, the energy field, the body. You, the true essence of you, can be found in all of it, bringing it to life, either freely or with distortions. Your soul essence is in every cell of your body.
2. The closer a layer is to this centre the closer its qualities are to your true self. So, the first layer, closest to the centre is the layer of joy. When you experience bliss, joy, laughter, play, creativity, love, abundance, wonder or fun you are getting closer to your true self. The outermost layer, the physical body, is furthest away from your true self. If you overly identify yourself as your body, you can become increasingly disconnected from who you really are and as a result, you feel a sense of dissatisfaction, a longing for more, for purpose and meaning, or a sense that you are missing something. Disconnected from your source, you seek to remove these feelings of dissatisfaction by looking outside of yourself. I'll be happy when_______ (fill in the blank) but joy is who you *are* not something you *get*.
3. Each layer flows through the outer layers. So, for example, you can experience bliss in your thoughts, your emotions, in your energy field and in your body. Likewise, a fearful thought will flow into your body

as a chemical cascade and result in tension, muscle contraction, changes to heart rate and breathing—everything plays out in your physical body.

4. As you move outward, the layers change from least dense to most dense. Think of the ethereal nature of thought versus the solidity of a bone, but it's all energy and all energy can become matter/stuff/things. It's quicker to change a painful thought than a physical pain, which is denser, so patience is essential.
5. All layers have dents and distortions from the life which shaped you so far. When it comes to healing, you can work on each layer at the same time, or just pick one at a time to work with. The more you can heal the dents closest to the centre, the faster you heal it all since the inner layers flow through the outer layers and influence them.
6. Think of each layer like a net, a series of nets. The nets trap debris, making it harder for the light of the soul to pass through. The nets can be cleansed but they'll tend to get blocked again, so the cleansing process becomes a lifelong daily practice, just like eating and sleeping.
7. The body is where we experience everything but by the time disease shows up here, there has already been disease at the deeper levels. Most people are disconnected from the wisdom of their embodied experience, what is happening inside them right now. Rather than address the deeper root causes of pain, they seek the remedy outside of themselves. They reach for a drug of some sort—pills, alcohol, surgery, work, sex and so on, something to numb the pain, but it doesn't go away.

Take a quick inventory of the current health of your layers by assessing some of the symptoms in each one (it is not a comprehensive list, just something to start you thinking).

Tick all the boxes which apply to you:

Physical Symptoms:

- Physical aches and pains ☐
- Physical tension and stiffness ☐
- Digestive issues ☐
- Immune problems ☐
- Skin issues ☐
- Hormonal issues ☐
- Diagnosed chronic illness ☐
- Fidgeting, can't sit still ☐
- Insomnia ☐

Energetic Symptoms:

- Fatigue/tiredness ☐
- Excessive/manic energy ☐
- Anxiety ☐
- Depression ☐
- Emotional overwhelm ☐
- Emotional shutdown ☐
- Having one dominant emotion ☐
- Breathing issues ☐
- Circulation issues ☐

Thinking Mind Symptoms:

- Can't switch off the mind ☐
- Can't focus or concentrate ☐
- Stuck in your point of view ☐
- Difficulty making decisions ☐
- Like to be in control ☐
- Need all the facts ☐
- Don't like surprises ☐

Habit Mind Symptoms and Sources:

People-pleasing	☐
Perfectionism	☐
Self-sabotage	☐
Strong beliefs you think are truths	☐
You don't believe you can change	☐
You believe you are what you are	☐
History of trauma and loss	☐
Had a chaotic childhood	☐
Had a controlling childhood	☐
Lots of childhood illness/surgery	☐
Victim of bullying	☐
Negative repetitive patterns that keep showing up	☐
Pattern of abusive relationships	☐
Low self-esteem	☐

The list is truly endless, these are just some of the indicators that there is healing to be done at this level.

Joy Symptoms:

Rarely experience joy	☐
Prioritise work over play	☐
Can't remember what used to bring you joy	☐
Deny yourself fun	☐
Don't believe you deserve joy	☐
Believe you are not creative	☐
See lack everywhere, rather than abundance	☐
Feel that life is a hamster wheel	☐

The more boxes you tick, the more you are living out of alignment with your soul's purpose. Symptoms showing up physically are rooted in the deeper layers, even the choice not to care for your body and its needs. So, even if you didn't tick many of the boxes other than physical, as you explore the topics in this book, you may start to bring to light some of the root causes of why you feel the way you do.

Before we dive into each layer, there are a couple of terms to introduce you to. The original text that brought us the kosha model was written in the Indian language, Sanskrit, and many of our own English words can be traced back to it as well.

The word for 'layer' is ***Maya Kosha*** and it's worth spending a moment on it. The word 'maya' has so many meanings and interpretations. It can mean 'illusion', that what you are seeing is not the truth. It can conjure up the image of a magic act, designed to trick you through sleight of hand. But 'maya' has no nasty, ulterior motive to deceive. It's playful and creative.

Another related meaning is 'to differentiate'. In this sense, it's like the ability of genetically identical human cells to look different and have specific jobs in the body depending on where they are…but they are essentially, at their core, all carrying identical DNA code and could have become any number of different shapes. Skin cells look and behave differently than nerve cells—this is maya. It makes the one creative life force able to assume an infinite number of different, seemingly separate forms. And yet *hidden* in the different appearances there is a core which is the same. The difference is the illusion. And the biggest illusion of them all is the sense that you are separate from everything else around you, cut off and cast adrift.

Just as the same DNA is at the core of all your different cells, the same core in me is in you and all of us, we simply inhabit different bodies, speak different languages, like different things and so on. The differences bring more variety to life, more beauty and creativity and are to be celebrated rather than stamped out. At our deepest core, we are all one and all connected, even if on the surface we all show up differently. When we view life from this perspective, from our heart and soul rather than our thinking mind, we *feel* this oneness. Deep down we sense our place in the whole. We all seek the same things—to be free to be our authentic selves and to express our feelings of love, joy and meaning without fear.

One more concept from the Sanskrit texts, and then we'll get into what this all means for you and your life. As I said in the introduction, the goal of this book is not to be academic but practical.

The source of all things, that oneness which we are each a drop of, is called ***Sat***—a difficult word to comprehend, it means 'that which truly is', absolute truth. It is—with no story, no value judgement. Simply something exists and is real. One of the ways I remember this word is to think of something 'just *sat* there' (not the best grammar but it makes the point). It's simply there, not doing anything just there, existing in reality. Neither good nor bad, it just is—like the lemon from before. Then we step in with labels and give them meaning. (In my opinion, one of the highest spiritual practices is to be able to view all things and all experiences, just as they are without attaching labels to them…for another book!)

Next is ***Chit***—this simply means that the thing is conscious—it's aware. Essentially, it's able to look out and perceive the world as well as receive information from the world and be aware that it is doing this.

For example, take a few moments and notice your thoughts right now. You can notice your thoughts because you are not your thoughts, you are the observer of them—that noticing, that awareness that you *are* noticing is chit (rather than the awareness of *what* you are noticing) and it's you at your core. So now you exist (sat) and you are aware (chit).

And last, but not least is ***Ananda***—this is another word with many meanings. It is soul force, power, creativity, agency, love, joy, and bliss. For me, what this word represents is that your true, free self has the agency (the permission and authority) to apply its power (energy and efforts) to create, share, expand and embody joy. There are an infinite number of possible ways it can do this and through you is just one of them. Whereas sat and chit are somewhat passive (an observer, sitting there), ananda is active—it's you beginning to move outward and ananda is your first layer.

You will often see words run together as **Sat-Chit-Ananda**: You exist, you are aware of the world and yourself, and you have the permission and the power to create the life you want, to explore and grow and to craft a life which allows you to experience *your* form of bliss. We are each a different drop of sat-chit-ananda and each of us can choose to craft our own satisfying but unique life. All the layers of your being are designed, when functioning properly, to bring the things you want to you.

Think of it this way—you are ***sat*** (eek! bad grammar I know!) in the driver's seat of your car with your hands on the wheel. Just sitting there. You become aware that you're sitting there holding the wheel and aware that you are at a crossroads with many possible directions—this is ***chit.*** Then *with a broad smile on your face* (this is key), you realise that you have the freedom to turn the key, put your foot down and drive the car in any direction you choose to go, at any speed and taking any route, and so, you do—that's ***ananda***! You may need to learn how to drive the car, which is the function of the thinking mind, but it's ananda that gets you into action.

Does that sound like the life you are currently living? If the answer is yes, then you can put this book away and get on with creating your magical life. If the answer is no, then I hope to guide you into starting to reclaim this life for yourself. Like most of us, you have allowed your unconscious, automatic programmes, rather than your soul, to make most of your choices, usually as an expression of some deep fear, rather than delight.

When you lose connection with the core truth of who you are, you consign yourself to the passenger seat. Instead of creating the life you want, your accumulated habits and the dysfunctional content of your habits and mind create your life for you…quite probably a life you don't want or like. By not being the creator of your life story, you give up your power and let others decide the kind of life you will lead instead.

Chapter 4
The Two Biggest Poisons of Our Generation

Nature does not hurry, yet everything is accomplished.
~ Lao Tzu

Before we dive into the layers, there is something to keep in mind if you want to cleanse your layers and find freedom.

In the last 30 years or so, our society has seen epidemic levels of chronic illness, including mental health decline, reduced resilience to life's ups and downs and off-the-scale levels of stress. In the same way that our habits and beliefs are so familiar that we no longer see them, as a society we have stopped seeing just how far away from our design we have become.

In our search for answers and remedies, we fall into the two familiar traps of modern life. I call them the two poisons: **complexity** and **speed.** We seem to overlook the blindingly obvious, adopting more and more obscure and toxic, so-called remedies. We stop trusting the innate inner intelligence to guide us, partly because it involves change and we tend to be averse to change at all costs.

Complexity

I grew up in the 1970s and 1980s. Back then, there were three ways to communicate if you wanted to have a conversation with a friend—the telephone (landline only), face-to-face or by letter. The post was delivered once a day, twice if you were lucky. Only one person could use the phone at a time, so if Mum was on it, I wasn't. Walking to see my friends took time and effort, as did writing to pen-pals, but it was an effort I was willing to make.

What didn't take effort because it didn't exist, was checking multiple messaging applications, every five minutes and being a slave to the constant pinging of notifications. I remember, back in the early 1990s, my housemate who was also called Claire and employed in the IT world, explaining these amazing new things to me—email and text messaging. I thought, '*That'll never catch on, why do we need that?*' Now we can't seem to live without them.

I had a similar conversation in the late 90s with an old college friend about the new internet. It was at a time when most of the world had no access to a telephone so I couldn't see how it could ever be more than a fad. But then smartphones and cheap mobile networks brought phones to everyone…and could we imagine living without the internet now? Ha, I'm clearly not a great predictor when it comes to IT—it's not my thing, so I leave it to others!

We have gone from three modes of communication to multiple messaging apps, text, voice messages, video conferencing, chat rooms, social media feeds and communicating through the medium of dance (what is that all about?) and probably many more methods I am blissfully unaware of. Trying to keep up with all the content (most of which is of zero value), the new versions and upgrades (so you don't feel left behind) is exhausting…unless it's your thing, in which case you'll think it's fun. But, for the rest of us, it can bring to the surface beliefs such as 'I can't keep up', 'I'm too old for this', 'I am failing', 'I am so busy', 'I'm no good' and many more.

Even something as mundane as ordering a coffee has gone from a choice of do you want that with or without milk to a three-page menu of options—it's bamboozling! Don't get me wrong, progress and innovation are wonderful things, especially when they level the playing field for all people. Having a choice is empowering; when we remember that we have a choice over *every* part of our life—not just how we take our coffee. We can choose to unplug our devices, delete apps and leave the phone in a drawer for the weekend…but do we make those choices? It's hard because we have become addicted to all this information, all this detail, all this complexity and we try to keep up with it all to avoid the uncomfortable feeling that we'll get left behind if we don't.

In the realm of our health and well-being, we do one of two things. On the one hand, we hand our choices over to someone else, because we can't see how to get back to health ourselves. We perhaps reason that we haven't studied medicine and health is something you need to get a degree in to be able to manage because health is complicated. So, we decide that it's somebody else's job to fix us.

Or, on the other hand, we micro-manage our health by obsessing over all the complicated details—blood tests, the calories or fat content of our food, supplementing with every vitamin and mineral known to man, trying out the latest fad remedy from eating just one food to poking around in our genome trying to discover which gene is 'faulty' and causing all this misery. At one end of the spectrum, we give up all ownership of our health and well-being, making it someone else's responsibility. At the other end, we try to fix everything ourselves, pushing away help and guidance and losing ourselves in the micro-details. One belief keeps us in the passenger seat, the other keeps us busy pouring over the car manual, trying to learn how a car works without daring to turn on the ignition and just drive it.

You don't see dogs and cats doing this, so why are we?

Then there is the complexity of daily life that comes from having to be all things to all people. It's not enough to be a full-time parent, we must also be on the school PTA, coaching the netball team, acting as taxi driver, homework supervisor and art project designer. That's before you add in the extra layers of competitive parenting, perhaps a full-time career outside the home as well as caring for an elderly relative. Something's got to give, and the chances are it's you.

Every time we feel a jolt of overwhelm or anxiety (also at epidemic levels in our society), it ramps up feelings of failing, falling behind, not being good enough, not being worthy, and being found out for these 'failings'. What do we tend to do when these feelings arise? We push them down, numb them and try *even* harder to keep up! This further jolts your nervous system and throws it into the fight-and-flight response, making you ready to defend yourself or run away and hide…all day, every day.

When we were living in the natural world, our nervous system developed to match the natural environment and it hasn't really changed since. Our nervous system was equipped to handle one jolt into the fight-and-flight zone about once every three months or so. I lived in the African bush for three years and contrary to what you might see on the telly, most antelopes are not bumping into lions every day. They may hear an odd noise, lift their heads to see what it is, realise it was just another antelope tripping on a stone and go back to munching grass. No drama and no rise in anxiety are needed.

Nowadays, your nervous system, which hasn't changed since the hunter-gatherer times of your ancient ancestors, gets jolted into the fight-and-flight zone eight to ten times *every day* on average (meaning for some people it's a lot more). That's a massive burden and a result of our complex and fast-paced culture. Breaking out of this cultural addiction is going to require a rebellious heart, a willingness to stop and say, “Hold on a minute, this isn’t working for me,” and the fortitude to forge a new way—the way of joy.

There’s another big barrier, right there. How good are you at stating your needs and putting them first? This is another belief you’ll need to unpick and it’s such a strong one, especially in women.

The remedy for complexity is **simplicity**. Our culture has come to define simple as ‘stupid, naive, unrefined, childish and inferior’. Simplicity is *actually* ‘elegant, clear, graceful, easily understood, causing no difficulty, free from the unnecessary and unspoiled’.

When you say the word ‘simple’, what meaning do you give it? How does the word and its meaning make you feel? Are you even able to tune into that feeling response? Don’t worry if you can’t—most people can’t at first. Relearning how to feel is how we can gain insight into our inner dialogue, the words we choose and how they impact us.

A healing medicine made from herbs was called a simple, years ago. In the Sanskrit language simplicity is ‘saucha’, often limited to ‘cleanliness’ and it is, sort of—a cleaning away of the unnecessary in our life. We clean our house regularly because dust and spiders gather if we don’t. We clean our bodies, so we don’t smell or get infections. How often do we cleanse our minds, our emotions, and our habits?

How did we let go of all this beautiful simplicity? And how can we reclaim it?

Well, some ideas to get you started might be:

- Commit to less—you’ll have to get more comfortable with the word ‘no’ but once upon a time, when you were two or three, it was your favourite word of all—reclaim that!
- Do one thing at a time, multitasking plays havoc with your nervous system and has been shown to be inefficient anyway.
- Reduce the amount of information coming at you and into you all day by deleting apps and turning off *all* notifications. Only check messages when you are ready to deal with them.
- Choose one social media app, and one messaging method and let the others go.
- Build space into your daily schedule—if you fill every moment of every day, you leave no room for the universe to weave its magic and then life

will feel devoid of mystery and spontaneity. You may need to address the resistance you feel and the beliefs you hold around giving yourself more space.

Doing one thing at a time is a good place to start. We've bought into the idea that we should all be doing ten things at once and if we're not then we're slacking, there's something wrong with us and we might get sacked. So, you try harder and keep doing more and more things at once.

The research is very clear—multitasking is inefficient. Even switching between tasks requires your entire brain to reorganise itself to cope. I know that if I want to be creative, writing this book for example, then I need a clear day, no admin, no accounts, no calls with clients. I need the headspace to let my mind wander, to receive magical downloads from the universe and then get typing.

I may only type for two hours but I have been in the creative process all day, without needing to switch to another part of my brain whilst I balance my bank account and switch back to creative thinking again. Switching and multitasking are exhausting and inefficient. An outsider may think I am being lazy or wasting time but I'm not and honestly, they can keep their opinions.

Now you might not be able to have entire days to devote to one thing but time-block your day wherever you can. When are you most creative? Do all your creative tasks then. When are you better at figuring things out? At communicating and answering emails? Match tasks with the energy and mental space that you are naturally in at different times of the day, and do one thing at a time. You will achieve just as much, if not more, with more grace and flow.

The thing that has worked the best for me (it might irritate people trying to reach me) is to remove all notifications on my devices and turn my phone to silent. I receive no pop-up messages and no pings. Every time a notification pings, part of your attention is pulled to it, along with some of your energy. You start wondering who it is and if it's urgent…you're no longer giving your full attention to the thing or person in front of you anymore. Not everything (in fact, almost nothing) needs to be responded to immediately. *Choose* when you will look at email, return missed calls and so on.

And this brings us nicely to the second poison.

Living at Breakneck Speed

I used to have a pen pal when I was a child and received a letter from her every couple of months. I would wait a few weeks to reply, filling her in with all that I had been doing. We were content and satisfied with waiting. In fact, it added to the joy of receiving her letter in the post when it did come, partly because it was never expected.

My generation, born in the 1970s or before, is truly blessed compared with the younger generations, for we lived through those years of simplicity and endless time. We remember it, it's in our bodies, and our body responds with good feelings of recognition when we allow ourselves to experience it again, right now. For those born into the age of speed and technology, speed feels normal to them because it's familiar. However, their ancient nervous systems are under constant bombardment for which it wasn't designed. They almost need to be taught how to slow down because it is not in their memory bank. No wonder so many young people are struggling with mental health issues right now.

These days, we are expected to reply to a text immediately. If someone doesn't reply to us within seconds, our internal storytelling goes wild—what have I done? Have I upset her? Is she cross with me? She is so annoying, why doesn't she reply? Well, if that 'she' is anything like me, maybe she left her phone at home today, for some peace…it's nothing personal but we make it so.

Waiting for connection wasn't something that used to cause stress. We didn't spend all day agonising about it in our minds. We went out and called on our friends and if they weren't home, we didn't take it personally. We have built up a huge wall of expectation and instant gratification. We find it so hard to sit in the space, in the emptiness before a reply without polluting it with our own drama. We want the reply to come in the way we see it in our head, no surprises. All this speed has robbed us of our patience and peace as well as our attention to what is *actually* happening right now because we are living out a fiction. Buying into the 'urgency culture' just keeps our nervous system ramped up and our stress responders on high alert.

We have the same addiction to speed when it comes to our health. We want the one magic pill that will take away all our symptoms right now, one visit to the therapist to cure our mindset. We expect to get on the scales after one day of eating well and see all our extra weight vanish or to be able to run five km after one session in the gym. With our addiction to instant gratification and urgency, we prize the finish line over the process of getting there. 'In process', by definition, isn't there yet so it amplifies our belief that we are not good enough. We think that only when we 'get there', wherever 'there' is, will that belief dissolve and we will finally be perfect. However, life is a process, for which the end destination is death. Don't rush to get there without truly living first.

We know this race we're in is all bullshit, but the pull of our habits, and what everyone else is doing, keeps us stuck on the hamster wheel. We do more and more and more of the things that keep us stuck, afraid of being left behind. After all, it's the antelope at the back of the pack that gets taken by the lion, so the body's fear is real. Are we failing whilst everybody else is happy? Um, no.

Stop! Get off the hamster wheel, slow down and take a breath. Take ten breaths. There is nowhere to get to, other than where you are right now. You are missing the beauty and joy of your own life because you are so busy rushing to get to some mythical future 'there' which does not exist. Existence is happening right now in front of your eyes and at your fingertips; stop pursuing fairy tales.

There is no magic pill, no magic cure, no quick fix, or fast-track to where you're trying to get to. Change occurs not through one dramatic gesture (although dramatic events can certainly initiate change) but through small boring acts repeated regularly. Healing is the art of unbecoming everything you have accumulated that is not your true self and it's a **practice**. In the Sanskrit language, practice is *abhyasa* and it's basically your habits. In many of the old yoga texts, we are reminded to practise with attention. You can either intentionally decide your habits of thinking, feeling, and acting, or you can leave it to chance, which means the past, someone else, or the world in general, is deciding your habits for you. It's the difference between being in the driver's seat and the passenger seat.

If you choose to live intentionally, with joy as your guide, tap into the creative energy of your soul, then **slow down** and stop rushing, so that you can feel and observe more. This may well mean you have to commit to less, which is a good thing because it will help to unravel the first poison of complexity as well as speed.

Learn to do less but with greater attention and mastery. I have been living with the knowledge of the koshas for more than twenty years now. The wisdom of this model has been percolating in me and through me for all that time. I have been exploring the world and myself through the lens of this model and other models too. Only now do I feel the alive spirit of it, know it with enough depth, in every cell of my body, to be able to live it and share it in a simple and accessible way. Albert Einstein said, *If you can't explain it simply, you don't understand it well enough*. It took me twenty years to come to my understanding and embodiment of the koshas and how to heal them within my modern life, and I'm still learning. This book is just *my* interpretation, at this point in time, and I hope in its simplicity it conveys clarity.

I once led a group transformative breathwork session and had the most interesting feedback from one woman. She shared at the end that she felt much more relaxed and peaceful (a good thing, right?) but she sounded disappointed, even a bit cheated, as she said that she had expected it to be more complex. See how deeply attached we have become to complexity? Even our relaxation should be complicated!

I am not merely being nostalgic in this chapter. I am a great advocate for evolving and changing things if they are no longer fit for purpose. Our addiction (yes, it is an addiction) to these two poisons does not serve any of us anymore and needs to change because the complexity and the breakneck speed we are expected to live at, are making us sick.

You *can* forge another way for yourself, as I have, and many others have too. But it will require some rebellion, a dose of bravery and a willingness to give up the collective addiction. If you don't believe you are addicted to speed and complexity, try giving them up for a week. You could go a week without your phone, decide on one messaging app and delete the rest, say no to every request, or limit your activities to two per day…pick one of these suggestions and try it just for a week, noticing the feelings that come up. Chances are your feelings may be really uncomfortable, and you'll want to reach for your distraction again. You'll find it hard at the beginning, if not impossible, and the length of the beginning is different for everyone, but if you can stick with the experiment you will start to love and crave the lack of rushing because it's your natural state. It gives you the time and space to rest back into who you truly are—joyful, loving, curious, creative, and free.

The remedy for modern life is simple but that's not the same as easy. The pull of your habits, beliefs, past traumas, and the collective pull of society will all fight you. Keep doing the simple things even, and most especially, when it all feels hard. Make it a practice because every day you are prone to falling into the pull of old ways or into the pull of the matrix of modern life and what it says you *should* be doing. Make healing a daily practice.

I do not recommend trying to change everything at once. Choose one new habit and do it every day for a month, or longer, as long as it takes until you feel you've mastered it. Remember, you have your whole life to master this, there is no rush. Once you have mastered the first thing, add the second, again do that for a month until you feel you've mastered it.

Healing is not a one-off event—anyone can commit to that. Healing is a daily commitment, being willing every day to say, "I choose to do the things which refresh, rebuild, and re-inspire me. I choose to slow down and simplify my life."

Healing is also a willingness to be with the opposite feeling without becoming lost in it. When things feel tough, when the urge to give up is strong, it is holding the vision that this isn't who you truly are, and to take those small steps forward, however tiny. Recommit to you every day.

Starting to change can be hard. Old habits are strong, and you are likely to feel worse before you feel better. I only drink two small coffees a day with my breakfast, I wasn't addicted as such. When I decided to take a few months off coffee I thought it would be a walk in the park. I had three days of horrendous headaches, and I knew a coffee would take it away, but I also knew this feeling was temporary. I had made a decision to be coffee-free, so I persevered. Perseverance is to be in the practice of recommitting to what your soul wants, not what your old habits want, every day.

And if you fall off the wagon, which we all do, never mind. Recommit and pick up where you left off. It's not about perfection, it's about practice.

If resistance is strong in you, first ask yourself if this change is what you *truly* want, or what you think you *should* want. Then, if it is what you want, give yourself permission for it to be easy and fun, which leads us nicely into the first layer.

Part 2
The Expansive Body of Joy – *Ananda Maya Kosha*

Chapter 5
You Are Powerful Beyond Measure

Our deepest fear is not that we are inadequate.
Our deepest fear is that we are powerful beyond measure.
It is our light, not our darkness
that most frightens us.
~Marianne Williamson

Ananda is a wonderful word—literally! Your soul came here to shine but like all of us, you gathered beliefs and fears around how safe it was to be the radiant, powerful human you truly are. To fit in with the masses, you turned down the dial on your brightness and settled for less. No wonder so many people reach a point in their lives where they feel lost and go off to try to 'find themselves' again.

Your soul came here with its own personal loves, desires, and talents. It came to fill a gap that until your birth had been empty because life was waiting for you. It's as if you are the final piece of the jigsaw and without you, the whole picture doesn't come alive.

Just as every jigsaw piece is a unique shape and colour, so are you. The purpose of your life is to be the piece you were born to be and find where you fit the best. If you're a jigsaw piece with two holes and two nobbles, stop trying to be an edge piece—that's someone else's role. One of my favourite yoga texts, *The Bhagavad Gita,* teaches: "live your own life however imperfectly, rather than someone else's perfectly." It's telling you to stop imitating others and receive the gift of who you are. A good mantra to live by but how many of us really do that?

I think the main reason we look at others and want their life is because it's easier to copy than it is to create. Creating your own life, being authentically you, means embracing the unknown—who are you? What will it be like to step into the unknown? You have never existed before, there is no manual to follow, you are a pioneer in your own life adventure.

Imitating others makes the future predictable and avoids having to feel the fear of the unknown, but it leads you to merely repeat the known, which is absolutely fine if you are living a life of joy and fulfilment, but if you sense you want more for your life, it would be a good idea to let go of the need for predictability. You are not a photocopier; you are an artist.

Remember what I said about the day you were born? Everything was unknown that day but back then you were fearless, and you allowed yourself to embrace the unknown and explore. You learned about what you liked and what you didn't. You learned what lit your soul on fire and what was dull and uninspiring. No child will voluntarily spend time doing dull things, they play at what they love.

Why did we stop?

We got programmed and we got scared. We wanted to fit in, be loved, be accepted, be seen and so on. We learned that receiving love was conditional on us behaving in a certain way. We started to try to engineer how other people saw us and valued us, and we started to try to control as many things as we could in order to feel safe, loved, and accepted.

I think most of us lost touch with ananda somewhere along the way and those who didn't, stand out like superhumans, fearlessly charging through life doing what they want, totally themselves, achieving great things and we watch them…and feel even more inadequate. Social media has massively amplified this comparison addiction and the feelings of unworthiness it brings. We look at people presenting their enviable lives online, but we don't see the forty-nine photographs they rejected to settle on the 'good' one. We see the perfect restaurant meal but not the pile of junk food cartons in their rubbish bin. Back in the 1980s, we had only magazines to compare ourselves with abnormally tall and slender women to make us feel unworthy (ignoring the fifty people in our actual world who were the same height and build as us). Today it's a daily assault, coming at us constantly. Stop comparing your real life with someone else's online fictional life.

Imitating others can be a helpful first step to discovering who we are and what we love. A mentor of mine once said what we admire in others and what we are jealous of in others, is what we have but are not using in ourselves. Wallop! That hit me like a punch in the gut, such a deep truth. Who and what brings up feelings of admiration and/or jealousy in your life? Who would you want to imitate? Can you own the fact that you have that gift within you already, but fear is stopping you from stepping in and claiming it?

Our fears are lodged in the second layer but let's explore what it is we are trying to reclaim in the Ananda Maya Kosha. In Chapter 3, I defined ananda as soul force, power, creativity, agency and bliss. Think of it as light. When you turn on a light it radiates out and fills the room. It doesn't hide in a corner, it shines out, unashamedly and unconditionally. It doesn't worry about whether or not the world will like its light. That's the spirit of ananda.

Just like light, ananda is energy, its raw power, it's a force. Ananda is your soul's empowerment. It comes to life the moment you turn the key in the ignition, press the accelerator and let go of the brake. That moment is either full of excitement or full of anxiety depending on the content of the second layer, but at a soul level, anxiety and excitement are both the same energy. Right before your stories claim it is as good or bad, it is just pure aliveness. Maybe you can feel it in your chest right now as your heart resonates in recognition of these words. Notice if you jumped to label the feeling exciting or scary.

There are many different energies and feelings which naturally flow outwards, expanding and moving you into the world, connecting you with the people and environment around you:

- Unconditional love
- Wonder and curiosity
- Infectious joy
- Desire
- Gratitude

Ananda has no doubts or expectations because it exists entirely in the here and now, the present moment, just as it is. Doubts are a legacy of past experience being projected onto today's decision. Expectations come from the future, what we think the outcome should be. But ananda only exists now. In this way, it's spontaneous, free, curious and doesn't know the outcome, but it trusts itself. It knows deeply that it is capable of meeting whatever comes.

Depending on the content of your second layer—your beliefs—this idea of spontaneous freedom may bring up images of recklessness, immaturity, selfishness, and even foolishness. It might bring up a statement that says it is for other people, but not for me.

On the other hand, the idea of spontaneous freedom may feel liberating, hopeful, even exciting. The labels you assign have nothing to do with this pure energy. Somewhere in your past, you learned to assign these labels and in doing so you create your personal relationship with freedom and whether or not you welcome it into your life. Your soul force is a raw material, your beliefs either block it or direct how you use it in your life.

Think of ananda as your potential. Just like the potential energy locked up in a battery, it's there waiting to be plugged in and put to use. A battery is a completely pointless object on its own but when put to use its value is revealed. You have so much potential, and you also have agency—choice about how you want to put that potential to use, and how much of it you want to bring to life. There is no judgement here. Your soul doesn't judge you for not using all your potential, but it's there waiting for you if you choose to claim it, or even just some of it.

Ananda incorporates so many elements that you may have been told are *not* to be pursued—welcome to the ant colony, be the same as everyone else. No, welcome to the jigsaw. We have reached a time in human evolution where we are stepping out and up. Out of the collective trap we have all fallen into and up, becoming lighter, freer, and more creative. This is happening all around us as we see old structures, old ways of being dissolving, so much innovation and creativity all around. You are being invited to break out of the confinement of trying to live *down* to someone else's ideals, so often based on fear and lack, and allow your radiant heart to lead your way.

I use the words soul and heart interchangeably. Many people believe the soul is located in the heart. In the energy map of the body, the heart is located dead centre and it is from the centre that we want to live—from the inside out. For centuries we have let the head lead, which is layer 3 in our Kosha Map. Now we are being invited to lead from the heart—the true centre of our being. The head is but an employee of the heart. The Kosha Map has been waiting for all this time for humanity to be ready to step in and live by it.

The world may feel chaotic and unpredictable right now but to live from ananda is to be able to trust that everything is happening just as it is supposed to, and we are not powerless. On the contrary, we have the power to choose how we will navigate this time of great change and what we want to plug our energy into creating. But we need to be willing to embrace the unknown for we are not being prompted to simply replicate what has gone before, nor do we need to put energy into fighting the process by clinging to the past. We can innovate and improve life for ourselves and for others by creating the life we want.

Okay, let me come back down to earth! It's so easy for me to ride that endless train of possibilities, but let's look at a few key attributes of the ananda layer one by one.

- Soul Power
- Curiosity and Wonder
- Desire
- Unconditional Love
- Creativity
- Joy
- Gratitude

Chapter 6
Soul Power—Get Back into The Driver's Seat

Your great power lies not on the surface,
But deep within your being.
~ Roger McDonald

Now this may not be what you want to hear but stay with me—you are in charge of your life. If you don't claim it, someone else will and you will be enslaved.

Reclaiming the driver's seat of your life is hands down the biggest (and perhaps hardest) thing you need to do, but you absolutely can—soul power is not something you have or don't have, it's who you are.

Several squirmy feelings arise around the word power. Collectively, we have been lulled into the belief that power means power 'over'. We may think of power in terms of the bully, forcing their agenda and everyone else being powerless, bowing their heads in submission. And let's be honest we see a lot of this still being modelled in the world right now. We have so few role models of heart-led leadership that we can indeed think this is the only way power exists and in response, choose to reject our own power as an ugly thing we want to be shot of—a form of self-abandonment. But power by force fizzles out, it is unsustainable as history always shows us—all regimes eventually crumble.

True leadership starts with yourself. Can you lead yourself to show up in the world the way you really want to? Can you show up as the very best version of yourself that you can access today? When you fall off the wagon, can you climb back on? Once you can lead yourself, others will *want* to follow because you embody integrity. Only when there is an absence of integrity does a person need to express power *over* another, to force others to their way.

True power is *for yourself.* Can you decide how to use your abundant soul energy and how you will keep your energy and integrity strong? Can you be intentional about how and where you use your power for your own highest good and, as a result, for the good of others?

Your power lies in being free to simply ask, what really lights me up and expands my energy? How can I do more of that today?

Another squirm you may have around the word power is related to how easily you give your power away…the opposite of the bully—the victim in this distorted dynamic. The unworthy one. Believing all power is bad or believing you are weak—these are just beliefs, and they are embedded in layer 2—they are not who you truly are, merely something you have accumulated. This is not to say that some people don't abuse or hurt you, but you don't define yourself by another person's actions.

Here in the first layer, there is purity because there are no attached stories or judgements yet. Everything just is. We get trained very early on to surrender our power to another, external authority. Perhaps you grew up in a controlled and rules-based home where behaviour outside of the rules wasn't tolerated. As a small person you were trained, one way or another, to toe the line, a line set by other people. Then came school with another set of rules. Religion, work, culture and so on all added more and more external control. How often were you allowed to decide something for yourself, make a mistake and be forgiven, experiment, and do things your own way? When did it all become about what everyone else wants and you stopped asking, "Is this right for me?"

No wonder we become adults unskilled in expressing our own power, making a choice for ourselves and being afraid to assert ourselves. Or due to lack of practice, we wield power like a weapon from a stance of vulnerability, desperately trying to make our world feel safe. What is it they say? *Attack is the best form of defence.* Backed into a corner where we feel weak and vulnerable, we lash out. This is not the power of ananda, it comes from fear and like all fear-based structures, it is not sustainable.

Chapter 7
Wonder—The Mystery of the Unknown

He who can no longer pause to wonder and stand rapt in awe, is as good as dead; his eyes are closed.
~ Albert Einstein

To stand rapt in awe requires several things from us which, in our modern world, feel alien.

The first is to be still, stop doing, stop rushing and simply be present with what is happening right here and now. Modern life is too complex and too fast, we don't carve out still-time daily. Flopping in front of the telly exhausted every evening is not still-time, it's just numbing out your dissatisfaction, rather than pausing to receive the wonder of existence.

Living life in such a hurry, looking for a quick fix and bypassing the actual medicine your soul needs is a futile squandering of your soul force, to the extent it drains away, and you try even harder doing all the same wrong things to get life 'sorted'. Life isn't something to sort out, it's to be experienced and enjoyed!

When we rush to get to the end, we lose connection with the present moment. The end of our to-do list, our day…our life! Have you ever caught yourself saying, "I can relax when I've done all these things—the job, the laundry, the dishes, the garden, the accounts…blah blah blah?" When did you take ownership of this belief? Who gave it to you? Give it back.

Life is a work of art, something to be crafted not an eternal to-do list.

I chuckle to myself as I write that last paragraph because that was exactly where I was not that long ago. Busy trying to do all the things, be someone of value, create something substantial, make a difference in the world. I had made a prison for myself. In the very first session with my mentor, she suggested I stop doing everything. I was horrified, and my face on the zoom screen went white with fear. Um, well, maybe…once I have done these three things, I might be able to take a bit of time off…was my lame response. "No, stop everything and see what happens," was her instruction.

As it turned out, stopping doing was the best thing I had 'done' for a very long time. I have been fascinated with self-development and personal growth for most of my adult life and certainly for the past 25 years as I pursued a career in yoga, meditation and health coaching. And yet, I had fallen once again into my own fear trap of trying to prove my worth through doing, doing and more doing. Deep down, I was running on the belief that what I did was valuable, but I wasn't. This time I was determined to be free from the trap once and for all, so I stopped. My mind went crazy. '*What!*' was what mostly filled my thoughts. Boy, it was uncomfortable! But there was also a deep knowing within me that this was exactly what I needed. My mind was freaking out, but my heart knew I was exactly where I was meant to be. I was safe and supported by the universe. I could hold the duality of discomfort and trust at the same time without becoming lost in either.

I gave myself time to let go. To let go of everything that wasn't serving me and wasn't setting my soul on fire and I decided to give myself a full year. When I stepped off the 'doing treadmill', my eyes opened again and I started to daydream, to be curious about who I was and what I *really* wanted. Opportunities came to me out of the blue, exactly what I needed at the exact right time. I made space in my life to receive. To receive my intuitive prods, to receive my body's wisdom when it said 'yes' and when it said 'no'. I received guidance from mentors and really, I received glimpses of the full possibilities of what my life held for me.

As I slowed down and the perfect medicines arrived in my life at exactly the right time I was filled with dreaming and wonder again. It overflowed into everything, even the most mundane things. I became curious about what old, unseen programmes were running my life and how many I could upgrade or ditch. I became curious about just how little I could do in a day and still feel worthy because, until that point, I had gotten all my self-worth from what I *did*.

Are you willing to stop? Does the very thought of that make your face blanche as it did mine? If stopping completely feels a stretch too far, can you schedule some unstructured time during your week, ideally every day, just as you would schedule any other appointment?

It might look like spending an hour when you finish work before jumping into the jobs that need doing at home, to just sit and be. And I mean that—just sit and be. That's the definition of 'SAT'—your core existence. Switch off your phone, and your TV; no books. Just let your mind wander rather than numb out scrolling a bunch of stuff on your newsfeed that zones you out. You can have a cuppa but that's it—look at the view, take notice of where you are, let yourself daydream.

How often do you go for a walk by yourself, without music, no podcast in your ear? Just walking and being present with your environment. (Take a phone with you for safety but keep it in your pocket and don't look at it).

Can you be alone with just you and your surroundings, exactly as they are? You'll start to notice so much more, things you would ordinarily gloss over. Slow down and look at things, really look, turn them over in your hands, and taste something for several minutes rather than rushing your food.

How much beauty do you rush by every day because you have adopted the collective belief that life has to be hurried—the urgency culture? How often do you assume you know the answers because you don't really pause and look at the problem fully…resulting in making the wrong choice and having to backpedal? And there we find another feeling we like to avoid—the feeling of not knowing can make us feel very unsettled and vulnerable.

Being rapt in awe and wonder is to feel small in the presence of splendour. To admit 'I don't know' can bring up fear but no human mind can know everything and where is the delight in that anyway? I love science but I still cannot fathom how a jumbo jet gets off the ground. I just watch it in astonishment and that's enough for me. On the other hand, I didn't know what limiting beliefs were skulking in my subconscious mind, and I *did* want to know what those were—that enquiry was of value to me, so I pursued it.

Some questions are meant to remain unanswered, and others are invitations to explore more. Being in a place of wonder reminds us that we have a choice—when we meet something that we don't understand we can choose to: 1) disempower ourselves and say, "I don't know how to do that" (what's left unsaid is—and I never will know, so I can't do it), 2) learn about it (engaging our thinking mind layer) or 3) simply bask in the mystery.

The older I get, the less inclined I am to fill my over-full head with more facts. I have so many half-read books around the house because I lost interest in trying to stuff more into my brain (something I would never have done in the past—I had to finish a book!). These days, I just want to be in the experience of right now, just as it is, enquiring more deeply into the richness of the moment, waiting for the right response to arise by itself. Right now, is a place where my entire being is participating, all my layers, not just my thinking mind. I am happy with not knowing and it brings a deep abiding sense of contentment. This is a completely different feeling from the need for knowledge which comes from anxiety.

The cousin of wonder is curiosity and I use this whenever I experience fear. For me, wonder is like daydreaming and getting lost in the moment, but curiosity is wonder directed at a particular thing, a kind of focussed wonder.

When fear arises and I want to move forward, it can stop me in my tracks. I remind myself that fear is just me meeting my edge, the outer edge of my familiar experience or an old wound I jump to protect. Some people think the antidote for fear is courage—to make a big brave step into the unknown. That doesn't work for me because when I meet that edge again, I now have two fears—the original fear and the fear of having to make that big brave step again…it's why I only jumped out of an aeroplane once…but more on that later.

I find curiosity is a much better tool for meeting fear. I simply allow myself to be at the edge of fear and stay there, neither moving forward nor back, just curious to explore what the edge is, where it comes from, what it's inviting me into, what the growth might be and so on. I find when I meet fear with curiosity that it slows me down, I see all the old stories coming to life like 'You're a failure', 'You can never have what you want', 'People will laugh at you' and so on, but I don't act upon them. In the slow motion that curiosity invites you into, it's more like you meet the fear by befriending it, you extend your energy towards it. The qualities of the ananda layer are all about expanding out to meet the world, whether that world is outside you or within you. I only occasionally need to find courage, because through curiosity, the edge yields by itself, fear dissolves, defences are dropped, and I find myself naturally expanding into something new that's on the other side. Fear lives in your second layer, but curiosity settles you into the ananda layer, this first layer and this is what you want to direct your life.

To get started connecting with wonder and curiosity in your daily life, here are some suggested daily activities:

1. Put time in your diary to be alone—no devices, no books, no conversation, no agenda and just be. Be realistic about scheduling your time so that nothing and no one is likely to invade your space. It might be that you need to set your alarm 15 minutes early so you can get up before the house comes to life. Or commit to having a bath with the door locked every evening for 15

minutes. But remember—no devices, no books—just you and let family members know you are not to be disturbed.

If you are a writing type, spend a few moments journalling your observations afterwards—where did your mind go? In the beginning, out of habit, you'll probably be planning or rehashing your day, thinking about your to-do list, wondering if you're doing it 'right', worrying in general and so on. That's perfectly okay. With time, that will settle, and the space will open up to let your awareness roam freely. Notice where it goes, what comes up for you spontaneously and receive it without judgement.

2. Intentionally pause every time something makes you stop and stare—every rainbow, sunset, newborn baby, the overwhelming feeling of love as you watch your child sleeping, the perfect rose, a moving piece of music and so on. Don't simply rush on to the next thing, mentally record its appearance in your life. Pay attention to all the times you allow yourself to slow down, wonder and be filled with awe.

You will still get all your tasks done but with a much more soulful, appreciative energy. Wouldn't you rather flow through your day being all the roles you need to be, doing all the things and feeling the wonder of being alive as well? You can have both if you practise, don't let anyone tell you otherwise.

The thing about wonder and curiosity is that they can be both universal and personal. I think most people feel wonder staring at the vast night sky or a far horizon—that's pretty universal. But there are other things that are just yours. Maybe you're like me and can get lost wondering what it would be like to have a tail, or be covered in fur…okay, maybe not. For you, it's something else…maybe you wonder what it would be like to feel confident.

Allowing wonder and curiosity to flow through you again can lead you closer to the other aspects of this first layer that are much more personal and unique to *your* soul—the specific things that you love, and which bring you joy.

Chapter 8
Desire and Love

Desire entered the One, in the beginning.
~ The Bhagavata Purana

Everything in life is born of desire. You were born of desire. What you want, wants you and you are worthy of all you desire. Desire is such a misunderstood quality but it's your personal agency and is something you need to reclaim. Desire is so closely woven together with wonder, love, and joy when it comes out of the ananda layer of your being.

The trouble comes when your desires come from a sense of lack, feelings of unworthiness, addictions, and distorted power. When you want something, it's important to know:

a. Where does that want originate in you?
b. Which way is it flowing?

Desire that comes from your soul will lead you to live the life you were designed for, the one where you get to express your true authentic self, where you get to be the jigsaw piece that you are. It allows you to tap into the flow of abundance, exploration and expansion that runs through you from your source. You'll feel satisfied and relaxed by following these soul yearnings.

Desire that comes from a sense of lack, that there is something missing, and that you need to find something from outside of yourself to complete you, is not the desire we're talking about. It's tinged with anxiety, contraction and even shame.

True desire flows outwards and when pursued in a way that satisfies you first, it also serves the world. Desire is not about pulling something *towards* you. You cannot fill up your dents from the outside, only from the inside. Desire is the first stirring of action, it's like turning the key in the ignition and deciding to fire up the engine.

In essence, what you want, what you love and what brings you joy are the same thing. When I coach women, one of the first questions I ask is, "What do you want?" Not just material things or your career, but also how you want to feel, and who you want to be. It's astonishing how many people can't answer that question. So many people have become disconnected from their hearts and souls that they no longer remember what lights them up.

Desire entices us to move out into the world, expand into the potential awaiting us. We are beings of desire, every decision you make is to fulfil a desire, either consciously or unconsciously. When you say yes to one thing, you are saying no to every other thing and vice versa—when you say no to change, you are saying yes to maintaining the status quo in your life. Desire is what drives choice and choice comes from either being clear on what you want and growing into that, or continuing to protect your old wounds and remain the same.

From its Latin roots, *de sidus*, desire means *to draw down from the stars.* Oh, how good does that sound! Since every atom in the material universe is made from stardust, you and I included, then to desire is to draw something together, create with the raw materials of the universe…yep, that's happening when you desire a cup of tea—you draw together the raw materials—water, tea leaves, milk, fire, crockery and you create tea. It's pretty much instant so you trust it—you wanted it, and you had the power and materials to bring it to life.

The trouble comes when your creation takes more time, more materials and is dependent on the input of others—you want something and then you must be patient, the universe needs to reorganise itself a bit more to bring it to life, and so doubt creeps in. You start to believe that maybe you can't have what you desire and so you quit. Stay true to what you are creating in your life, and it will appear. Holding the vision of what you desire, and trusting that it's on its way, are your work. Not controlling, trying harder or forcing to make it happen, your way.

When we desire something, and the next day send out doubts and beliefs, such as 'I'm not deserving of it', or 'Good things never come to me', 'Everything I do is always a failure', we are giving mixed messages to the universe, so it cannot reorganise to give you what you want. The energy and trust behind the limiting belief feels more real to you, you have a library of evidence to back up your belief. Since you feel it as true, the universe takes this as your real desire and delivers you exactly that—failure, because the universe works in the currency of vibration—that's your feelings. So, now you are manifesting, very successfully, from your programming. For your deepest desires to appear in your life, you need to feel them as true in every cell of your body. You must embody them as vibrations before you receive them in form. Your soul desire needs to be more real to you at this moment than your limiting beliefs, doubts, and fears.

Chapter 9
You Are Boundless Joy

When you do things from your soul,
you feel a river moving through you, a joy
~ Rumi

This quote by Rumi sums up why so many people are dissatisfied and diseased. How many of us can honestly say we are experiencing a river of joy in our lives?

Most of us did feel a river of joy as young children, so when did we lose connection with our very soul and become cogs in a machine, working hard and paying bills? When did we trade joy as our guiding light for the belief that life has to be a struggle?

Reclaiming joy, when it has been missing in your life for many years can seem like an impossible challenge. You fall victim to the belief that joy is something you have, or you don't have; you deserve it or you don't. But here's the thing—joy isn't a thing. It isn't something to obtain, it's something you *express* from the inside out.

I love the word 'express'. If you look it up in the dictionary it has many meanings. In terms of food, it means to squeeze out the flavour within, such as the essence of an orange in its juice. It also means to put into words or gestures, something that is thought or felt inside, so that an experience can be shared. Finally, it implies something is fast and direct, as in the express train which makes no stops.

When you express joy through all that you do, even when life is squeezing you to the limit, you are allowing the first layer to support what your soul wants—to joyfully be itself. It's about allowing the uniqueness within you to be seen and shared with the world, regardless of what is happening around you, rather than hiding it away out of shame. And it's the fastest way to create healing in all the other layers of your being and your life.

Take a moment to consider this question, maybe answering in your journal:

When you go out in the world, do you censor yourself, hold yourself back or refrain from really being you, in case others either don't like it or worse, ridicule and reject you?

Honest self-inquiry will almost always answer with yes, and you can probably think of five ways you did it just yesterday. Maybe:

- You had the same old haircut, even though you would love to dye your hair pink.
- You felt like skipping down the road but held back in case people thought you were crazy.
- You wanted to say to the lady in the supermarket how beautiful she looked but held back because you didn't know her, and she might think you're odd.
- You wanted to use a word you really feel, like 'God' or a swear word but didn't because you were afraid the people around you wouldn't approve or would misunderstand you.
- You wanted to contribute to a meeting at work with an idea but held back because it might have sounded stupid.

This is the beginning of all your woes—a reluctance to follow your joyful and honest impulses. Desire and impulse are the same thing. Why is it so hard to give yourself permission to be yourself and follow those natural outflowing desires? Trust me, the world will never give you such permission—the collective culture wants to keep you the same as everyone else. But you are not an ant in a colony, you are a unique human being, and you have *permission* through your own agency to pursue the life you want.

What lights you up probably doesn't light up your neighbour, and nor should it, because they're not you and you are not them. You only need to venture into a newspaper or onto social media occasionally to see just how much pressure there is to conform, behave and speak a certain way. But the question becomes, conform with whom? If we are all unique, who gets to choose who we are all supposed to try to be like? It's nonsense and it's keeping you from living your life, your way.

During my twenty years as a yoga teacher and practitioner, I learned and taught the dangers of too much attraction and avoidance. The ancient teachings tell us that these extremes are the path to suffering. Whilst I agree to some degree (after all, addictions and chronic avoidance reside at these extremes) on one fundamental point I have a different perspective. We all have unique desires and preferences, and very often we have them for no logical explanation. I mean why do I love cabbage so much I could inhale it daily, but its smaller cousin, the Brussels sprout makes me recoil with revulsion. It makes no sense and I have learned not to question it, just follow it—I choose not to eat sprouts. I don't care how good they are for me; I do not like them even after years of trying. This is just a small example of the freedom and relief that can be released within you when you stop trying to do something that doesn't excite you because someone else is telling you that you should…so long as it's not coming from fear.

Attraction and avoidance are only problematic when they arise from feelings of lack, fear, and anxiety. Arising from the soul, your desires are your inner compass for a satisfying life.

You love what you love, you love who you love, and that can be your greatest guide to finding fulfilment in life. Now, I have been called a hedonist at times in my life. To be honest, I wasn't quite sure what that was, so I had to look it up! I discovered it's a person who is a pleasure-seeker. This is absolutely true! I do pursue what brings me pleasure but that is not the same as falling into addictions and living with wild abandon which results in my own ruin. In fact, I would say it's the opposite. I live very intentionally, following what lights me up inside because that is when I know I am living from my soul. Living from my soul is where I have the most positive impact on my life *and* the lives of others. Resentful servitude to societal norms serves no one.

Hedonism then, can be seen, not as debauchery, but living by design. By bringing the presence of mind and full body awareness to every decision I make, I make more fulfilling decisions rather than letting outdated beliefs, fears and the beliefs and fears of others make decisions for me. This was hard to accept as a yoga teacher because, sadly, there is a big culture of control, conformity, repression, and spiritual bypass within the spiritual community. Desire is so often misunderstood and simply labelled 'bad'. We are given the blanket instruction to avoid desire at all costs because it will lead to our downfall. After two decades of trying to squeeze myself into the yoga beliefs of the collective, I walked away from teaching…it was not bringing me any joy anymore and I was tired of fighting against the tide.

If, when making a decision, I don't feel the river of joy, then I do nothing. I have learned to *wait* until the right action arises by itself, from within and I feel that river of joy moving through my whole being. It feels like a full body yes! Waiting is so alien to our modern speed culture, but by not waiting we run the risk of knee-jerk decisions devoid of any contemplation and then having to backtrack to repair the damage.

> Here's a little exercise for you:
>
> Sit or lie comfortably for a few minutes and consider something you love doing. It might be painting, having a hot bath, playing tennis, sewing, sleeping in. Once you have the picture, allow yourself to visualise it in as much detail as possible, bringing in all your senses: colours, scents, textures, sounds and so on—what does it *feel* like when you're doing that activity?
>
> Hold the visualisation in your mind's eye and the feeling in your body as if you were actually doing it right now, for as long as you want to. Be in full presence with it and by that, I mean—be attentive to all the details of the picture and all the sensations in your body.
>
> Then, consciously invite the feeling to radiate out from you like white light in all directions. Take as long as you need to connect with this visualisation (it may take several attempts). When you are ready to come out of the visualisation, invite the feeling to come with you into the rest of your day.
>
> Make a note of any times in your day when this radiant, expansive feeling gets dented. What dented it?
>
> Also make a note of any times in your day when this radiant, expansive feeling arises quite naturally by itself. What were you doing at those times that allowed this feeling to flow through you?

Put a marker on this page to come back to and once you have tried it a few times, before you open your eyes, without forcing an answer, you can ask one more question of yourself:

What would you love to do, what do you really want for your life?

The answer might surprise and terrify you in equal measure, but here's the thing—that's in you, not me or anyone else. It's what *your* soul wants to express in this lifetime and it's inviting you to bring it to life. You can of course decline but it's yours to pursue if you want to. If you desire it at a soul level, you were designed for it.

So why don't we pursue what our soul wants?

Because of all the garbage in our outer layers, as you'll see in the next chapters. But your soul is saying yes, and your joy is confirming yes, but are you willing to align all the other dimensions of yourself with this desire and follow it? Most people don't. They die with their dreams still inside them because it takes persistence to do the inner work and not give up at the first hurdle. We have become a culture of instant gratification and quick fixes. Being willing to stick at something over time seems alien to us, especially when we look around and it feels as if we are the odd one out.

If you did this exercise and your answer was, "Nothing came up, I don't know what I want, nothing lights me up," then I am going to invite you to repeat this daily for at least a month. Be patient—it can take some time to connect with your intuition, your soul's voice and very often the answer is there but the mind so quickly jumps in to squash it that it can be easy to miss. Eventually, the answer will come, so long as you don't force it.

Don't panic—there is nothing defective about you. You were not left out when joy was being handed out. You have it, but you may have been disconnected from it for so long that it's hard to find, like looking for a needle in a haystack. But you *can* find it and when you do, you can release the river of joy and bring the pursuit of it into every day. For me, joy is in the act of pursuing something I want, connected to a desire that arises from within, not from any sense of lack. Following what you want is not about filling the holes you feel within yourself, it's about pushing out those dents from the inside. It's about expansion and connection. It arises from your fullness and abundance, and a belief that you are meant to do or have what you desire inside. You have the ability to make it appear, thinking you don't is a belief you received from someone else and beliefs don't exist in the ananda layer—they are not who you are, they are something you acquired.

I think it might be worth saying here that I do not go around all day long, laughing my head off like a hyena. It's not that kind of joy. It's a positive affirmation that comes from the deep knowing that I am alive, and I get to live all my experiences fully (the good, the bad, and the downright ugly). Nothing needs to be pushed away or bypassed. Rooted in joy, I can choose never to be a victim because I have a choice over how I want to feel, what I want to do and who I want to be. I used the word 'want' three times in that last sentence. It's the foundation of life. So, what do you want?

In this chapter, we used a visualisation of an activity that connected you with joy so that you could start to feel and explore it again. Using outside prompts to reconnect you with the feeling is fine in the beginning. But the ultimate source of your joy is your soul. We have all heard that happiness comes from within, it's not something you get and that's true, but at the start, anything which helps you to remember the feeling is useful. Eventually, joy is a state of being where you can be with everything exactly as it is, intentionally and authentically responding to it, free from stories or needing things to be any different than they are right now. In joy, you are happy to witness and experience life unfolding, just as it is and be in a state of wonder with it all.

Joy is a kind of allowing or accepting of how things are. Not in a defeated giving up kind of way where you step aside and let go of your power and desires. It's a contentment to be *with* things just as they are. It's a feeling of being able to hold even pain and discomfort with kindness because you know all things flow, and there is something for you in every situation. Sitting with pain is a gateway to healing those parts of ourselves we feel compelled to protect. Joy invites us into even more expansion. It is holding a patient, peaceful and inquisitive inner state, free from resistance. This absence of resistance creates space within you, and within your life, for things to do what they need to do.

Let me give you an example. You have a toothache and it's painful. Living in joy means also living in your own power, so you don't feel like a victim, lamenting, "Why is this happening to me?" Nor are you laughing about how wonderful the pain is, in a state of denial. You simply recognise you need to get some professional help, so you visit the dentist. The tooth is beyond help and needs to be removed. Again, you don't fall into a victim storyline, you are able to allow it all to unfold in its own way. You agree to have the tooth removed. Afterwards, your gum is sore for a week as it heals. Then you are free from pain. Even during the healing, you can see the greater benefit coming your way, you can accept the discomfort, knowing it's temporary and it is not who you are. Joy can look like calm peacefulness in the presence of drama unfolding all around you.

So how can you strengthen your feeling and experience of joy?

As well as the exercise above, I have a couple of tools for you that can act as the first stepping stones to the deep well of effervescent joy, love and wonder that is your birthright:

1. The Joy List Exercise
2. A Daily Gratitude Journal

Chapter 10
The Joy List Exercise

Find out where joy resides, and give it a voice far beyond singing.
For to miss the joy, is to miss all.
~ Robert Louis Stevenson

This exercise helps you to identify not only what you love to do but the deeper *feeling* that you have when you're doing it. Pursuing things you enjoy is not a selfish act (that's a belief in the next layer) because when you feel joy, it flows out of you, and you spread joy, which is far from selfish, it's generous. You know this to be true when someone, at an inappropriate moment, gets a fit of the giggles and you all try to suppress it, but within minutes everyone is laughing so hard the tears are running down your faces and the whole room is rolling about on the floor.

Joy is infectious.
Joy is the currency of connection and purpose.
Joy needs to be given a voice and shared, not buried.

Let's discover how doing what you enjoy can serve you and others in this exercise.

Joy Exercise Part 1:

In a journal make a list of 20 things you love to do. I suggest including some things which are free and some things you must pay for. Don't censor or judge your list—you get to enjoy whatever you like. It doesn't have to be logical or worthy and nobody else needs to see it.

For example, I love to hang out laundry to dry in the fresh air and I love the smell of it when it's dry. I also love to travel to tropical countries. As you can see, one costs nothing, the other rather more! But they both bring me joy for different reasons.

Now go back to your list and complete the second part of the exercise:

Joy Exercise Part 2:

Go through your list slowly, visualising yourself doing each one, and write down the specific feelings each item on your list awakens in you. You may have 3 or 4 words for each.

For example:
When I hang out the laundry I feel really ***grounded, present, humble*** *and* ***nurturing****.*
When I travel it awakens ***curiosity, exploration*** *and being really* ***alert*** *and* ***present****.*

Go through the list of words and notice which words come up repeatedly. You may end up with a shortlist of five to eight words. As you can see in my example, the word **present** comes up twice.

Follow your *instincts,* rather than logic, and pick two words from your list of recurring words. Write out a few ways that you love to express these two *qualities* both by yourself and when interacting with others.

When I first did this exercise my two words were ***creativity*** *and* ***curiosity.***

Many people are living dissatisfied lives because they are disconnected from their sense of joy and purpose. Their lives have become a dry routine, a living to-do list, disconnected from what lights them up.

We discover our purpose, not by looking forward and wondering if we will ever find it out there in the future, but by looking inward and backward. By looking at the things in your life that you have enjoyed, you can uncover the common threads running through all the things you've done.

I have always loved reading and being inquisitive, some might call it nosey even. It flowed through my years as a child, a student, a parent, a traveller, an experimental cook, a teacher, a coach, a writer. ***Curiosity*** is a strong thread in me, from loving a good whodunit novel to wondering what happens when I put my finger in a jelly whilst it's setting (answer: I get told off!), to diving into what makes other people tick!

I love finding ***creative*** new ways to communicate what I learn, ideally simplifying things and making them memorable. Interestingly, both feelings are aspects of the ananda layer, so when I experience either or both, I know I am coming from my soul's essence and that is where I want to come from.

When you reclaim what you love to do, you start to reclaim your joy. When you reflect on how doing what you love helps you feel satisfied *and* better connects you with other people, you have the beginnings of a sense of purpose and meaning. Now you must bring it to life by doing more of what you love. Give up trying to 'find your purpose' out there and instead choose to live *on purpose* right now by being authentically you.

Living on purpose brings you joy, and doing what brings you joy fills you with purpose—they feed one another, and it grows. No one who feels they live a life of purpose, even during challenging times, feels miserable at the end of the day.

You could stop reading this book right here and spend the next year discovering all the things that bring you joy, and then come back and carry on reading. If you are ready to explore how following your joy can also serve others, then keep reading.

Joy Exercise Part 3:

Go back to your two words from the previous exercise and insert them into this statement:

"My purpose is to do and share what I love. My purpose is to use my ___________ (word 1) and _____________ (word 2) to help others_________________________"

You get to fill in the final blank with what you love to help others to do.

It might be something you are naturally gifted at. For example, you might have a knack for finances, and you like to help others get out of debt. Or you might have an extraordinary gift for art and love helping to uplift others with your artwork…only you'll know.

If you are really struggling, ask a few people who know you well, what you're good at. Their answers might really surprise you. We often overlook our gifts because they come easily to us. We fall into the common belief that only what we have had to struggle for, holds value. This couldn't be further from the truth! Take your time with this, it doesn't need to be rushed, nor does it need to be perfect.

Once you have a rough statement, write it out several times, allowing the actual words that you finish the sentence with to subtly change each time. You may need to do this 10 times or 100 times, but eventually you will write something from the heart, rather than the mind—something that elicits an a-ha moment, an 'Oh, my God, yes—that's it!' moment.

Don't stop until you get there—it takes as long as it takes, but it's worth it.

One thing to note is the universe doesn't compartmentalise life into work, leisure, family etc. It's all life and your purpose can be found in all of it. It might be that currently, your career is not bringing out the best in you, but you feel your purpose in social situations or when you're alone. Over time, it is possible to bring the best of you to every situation, even change course and reorganise your life so that your purpose is given the opportunity to shine through everything you do if that's something you want.

This isn't an academic exercise. Go out and live this statement in small and large ways every single day and your life will be filled with satisfaction and meaning. Ask yourself, "How can I be in the spirit of creativity and curiosity (my two words) today?" Get into the habit of writing it out daily, reciting it to yourself as you shower or walk the dog. Print it out and stick it on the wall above your desk. Allow it to soak into yourself and become the essence of your life.

Give yourself permission to do what you love doing and be who you love being, and watch your life, your health, your work, your finances, your relationships, and your spiritual connection all improve way beyond what you have allowed yourself to settle for so far.

When I did this exercise a few years ago, after about 30 or 40 iterations of my statement, I landed with such clarity on:

'My purpose is to use my curiosity and creativity to help people shed everything that's holding them back from living the life they want.'

...I include myself in 'people' since I still have much to shed...and a few career changes of direction, have brought me to this point in time, and the desire to write this, my second book. One year ago, I hadn't written anything, I was too scared, and I kept coming up with excuses and now I have one book published, this one on the way, and the seeds of a third appearing in my mind's eye. More importantly, I love my life!

Your life can change as well…from night to day…but not without tapping into the extraordinary mobilising power of joy.

Go back to your original list of 20 joys. This list isn't all there is, so feel free to continue to add to it, especially joyful activities that are free. Your invitation is to do at least one thing every day that brings you joy, even if it's only for five minutes. The advanced practice is to bring the spirit of joy to tasks you don't currently enjoy, like cleaning the oven or doing your accounts. Think about how you can reframe these activities to bring more meaning to them, and how they serve your life in a positive way.

Chapter 11
Gratitude Practice

It is not joy that makes us grateful.
It is gratitude that makes us joyful.
~ Anonymous

Oh boy, I resisted this for years! I didn't believe something so simple could have so much impact and I was too busy. I wish I had listened sooner, but for the past four years, this has been a regular practice for me. It has had such a profound impact on how I have been able to navigate all the changes in my life during that time—COVID lockdowns, not being able to see my son for 13 months, emigrating, healing the symptoms of my autoimmune disease, changing my career—twice, and deciding to adopt a nomadic lifestyle in the middle of a pandemic, with most of the countries we wanted to visit, keeping their borders firmly shut.

Now I have put it down on paper, it looks totally insane! But it's been fun and challenging, but mostly fun. The ability to navigate some huge challenges without giving up or losing heart, I attribute to a daily gratitude practice. Yes—really! Scientific studies are now backing it up: gratitude makes you more adaptable and resilient.

It is normal for us to experience a negative bias in life. This is a natural survival strategy. If we were still living a tribal lifestyle, hunting and gathering out in nature then a part of our brain, our survival brain would be constantly scanning all the input from our beautiful environment coming in through the senses, ready to bring to our attention anything which doesn't 'fit'—"Hey, this could be a threat, take a good look." In the vast and beautiful landscape, it would detect the lion stalking you. This is good news because it brings the lion to your attention so you can escape to live another day. The survival brain is on the lookout for what's 'wrong', out of place and a danger to you. The survival brain was only triggered to make you run about once every three months. In modern life, it's being triggered eight to ten times a day.

You may not need to be on the lookout for lions on your commute to the office, but your survival brain is still functioning the same way: on the lookout for threats and there are more of them, real and imagined than ever before. Traffic, deadlines, being able to pay your bills, the news, avoiding getting fired, being acceptable, being rejected, have I got the right outfit on? It all feeds this same survival part of you. Over time, your negative bias becomes massively exaggerated and you view life through the lens of negativity—life is 'wrong' and that's all you see. Combine this with the kind of early programming you received around whether the world was a wonderful place or a dog-eat-dog world of struggle and you can get stuck in a negative mindset, focussing on what is wrong with your life and what in turn is wrong with you.

Practising gratitude is one of the quickest ways I have found to break the negativity bias. It's not about creating a Pollyanna outlook on life and saying, "It's all fabulous," whilst inside you can feel yourself rebelling against that. Good and bad both exist in the world, so this practice redirects you, so you don't *only* focus on the negative, whilst zoning out the positive.

We can programme our inner radar to focus on whatever we want. You know this to be true, I'm sure. If you decide you want to buy a new car and you set your heart on a bright red mini, you'll start noticing them everywhere. You didn't notice them very much until your heart told your mind they were important to you, so now every time your mind spots one, it brings it to your attention, until you decide, flipping heck I don't want a red mini now, everyone has one!

In the same way, you can programme your inner radar to disentangle from always showing you what's wrong, and start showing you what's right in your life. Remember, the world contains it all—the good, the bad, the old, the new, the familiar and the surprising. Through gratitude, you can become much more open to all the good things you have in life.

You may have become stuck in survival mode due to relentless, unattended stress, and a tendency to keep pushing through. Your negativity bias leads you to close off in a desperate attempt to self-protect. You become isolated from other people and your connection to something bigger—the source energy of the universe which runs through you, as creative, joyful self-expression. Being stuck in survival mode fixes your mind to be set on the belief that everything is hard, and the world is something you need to fight and defend yourself against. You become a victim, and you start reacting to life coming at you, rather than designing it for yourself, forgetting that you are a creative being. You stop living from the inside out and instead, face each day as if going into another battle.

Have you ever woken up and said to yourself, "Just get through today or this week or this month and then things will settle down?" Then off you go, head down, shoulders hunched to fight your way through another day.

Consciously creating a positivity bias doesn't mean all negative events leave your life. What does happen, is you're able to hold those negative moments within a larger container of goodness which in turn allows you to be with difficult times and difficult emotions without becoming overwhelmed by or stuck in them. This is a major aspect of healing—you cannot heal a wound until you're willing and able to *feel* it. Only then can you let it go and move on. Being able to be with old traumas, feel them, and allow them to complete the process of moving through you which got interrupted and then stuck, can only occur successfully in a container of safety—a deep, embodied knowing that no matter what happens, you are okay, and everything is happening *for* your benefit, there is growth available here. Safety cannot truly exist when you are stuck in survival mode, on the lookout for the next threat.

Studies have shown that physically, gratitude works by increasing the tone of the vagus nerve—one of the largest nerves in the body, not dissimilar in size to your spinal cord. The vagus nerve branches out and connects with most of your internal organs, especially your gut and your heart, and is responsible for checking in with how you feel in your whole body, about your environment and your place in it, moment to moment. Most of the information flows from the body to the brain. Your body knows how you feel about something (whether you are experiencing a friend or a foe) before your mind does.

The vagus nerve has a major influence on digestion, rest and social engagement. Being able to connect socially reaffirms that you have support and that you are safe and well-resourced to meet danger. Social isolation, on the other hand, has been shown to have as much of a negative impact on long-term health as smoking. I know from working with people with chronic illness, just how common digestive disturbance, insomnia, fatigue, and stress are in our society. It's a silent epidemic and whilst it's very common, it is *not* normal.

When the vagus nerve is in good shape, it brings your three 'brains'—your head, your heart and your gut into coherence. They become in tune with each other and therefore harmonious. When you don't feel harmonious, it's a sign to get back into connection with your body.

There is far more information coming from your body to the brain than from the senses bringing in information from outside of you. Every cell is an antenna picking up the quality of where it finds itself. The body is a massive source of information, wisdom and truth, and cutting yourself off from it to live entirely from your head, thinking and planning your way through life, trying to control everything, is to significantly limit your potential. Yet most people are doing exactly that—living from the head, ignoring the body and as a result, struggling through their lives.

Make the decision that it stops today!

Practising gratitude brings you back into connection—with your body, with your intuition, with your heart, with other people and with your source energy which is infinite and abundant.

The science of gratitude practices has been shown, over time to:

- Improve your general health
- Reduce inflammation
- Improve your food choices towards more nourishing options
- Improve heart health and lower blood pressure
- Improve sleep and general relaxation
- Improve digestion
- Make you more resilient to stress

Create the habit of feeling gratitude for what you have and desire for what is coming. They go together. If you cannot be grateful for the things you have now, however small they are, you won't be able to manifest more. If you give someone a small gift and they show no appreciation for it, simply toss it aside, how inclined will you be to give them another, bigger gift? The Universe works the same way.

So, let's look at how to do it…it's so simple but don't let the simplicity fool you—it's powerful.

Ideally, do this first thing in the morning, setting your alarm just 15 minutes earlier. If you don't get to it first thing, never mind just make a promise to your well-being that you will get to it later, even if it's at bedtime.

1. Start by taking a few minutes to close your eyes, and observe the in and out flow of your breath. Feel the support underneath your body and invite the body to soften and relax. Slow down and become more receptive and attentive. Take as long as you need and if it helps, play some relaxing music.
2. Write a list of ten things you are grateful for. If this feels really hard at first, then start with three and build up. Building your capacity is not unlike building your biceps at the gym—you'll get stronger the more you practice.
3. Express in writing *why* you are grateful for that item on the list. This isn't just a list-writing exercise, something else to tick off on your never-ending to-do list. You want to *feel* the gratitude in your body. You want to positively change your energetic state. Once the joy and gratitude are flowing, you bring that into everything you do and every encounter you have all day long, which is why I like to begin my day with it. Once your energetic state feels better, you are living from the inside out.

That's it—so simple!
Let's address some common questions:

- *Do I have to write it, can't I just think about it?*

Yes, you do have to write it in longhand. There is a power in writing far greater than just thinking about it. It engages more regions of your brain and is literally changing how your brain is wired which builds new neural pathways for future resilience; it's the fast-track to hardwiring gratitude into your life. You will reach a point (more quickly by writing) of living in a state of gratitude most of the time, so that even challenges, which other people might be tempted to pity you for, do not feel overwhelming to you.

- *Can I type it, instead of writing it longhand?*

No. There are several benefits that handwriting has over typing, including:

- Handwriting uses more parts of the brain, particularly those associated with language, healing, thinking and memory.

- Handwriting sparks creativity (an ananda quality) in part because it's slower, giving you more time to process thoughts and creates space to develop new ideas.
- Handwriting invites brain-dumping, which in turn helps you to organise ideas, spot patterns and draw connections. This helps you to break out of automatic behaviours and again, invites creativity and the possibility of change.
- Handwriting relaxes the mind. It's a mindfulness practice, similar to doodling or painting, bringing you into a state of peace rather than chaos.

- *Does it have to be ten?*

Well, no. But to go back to the bicep-building analogy—more repetitions bring better results, so if you just want to do one then that's up to you but find a number that works to shift you more fully into a grateful vibration. It's important that it doesn't feel like a burden though—you don't want that energy radiating through you! How many items does it take for *you* to feel gratitude buzzing inside?

Here are some of my top tips:

1. You can be grateful for things in your life that you have, things you experience or how you feel. For example, you might feel grateful for your home (a thing), lunch with a friend (an experience) or the freedom you feel from walking your dog in the sunshine (a feeling).
2. You can pull from the past, present, or future. For example, gratitude for your favourite teacher at school who supported you to get where you are today (past), the sound of the birds as you write in your journal (present) and for the new job you are attracting to you now (future). Yes, you can be grateful for the things you are intentionally calling into your life that haven't arrived yet! This is a wonderful expression of trust in an abundant universe.
3. Try to have some new things each day, rather than writing out the same list day after day—this is not school detention where you were assigned lines as punishment. Remember this practice is to enrich your life.
4. You can be grateful for the same thing or person every day but come up with different reasons why you are grateful for them. For example, I am grateful for my husband every day, but the reason changes and this deepens and strengthens my connection with him and my appreciation

of him. Sometimes it's because he makes me tea in the morning, sometimes because he sorts out the internet when it goes wrong, sometimes it's his enthusiasm to live life so differently than other people—the list is endless.

5. On special occasions, you might dedicate your entire list to one thing. For example, maybe on your son's birthday, you list ten things you are grateful for about your son and why he is so important to you.
6. Take a few minutes at the end of the day to read back what you wrote that morning, close your eyes and rest in the deep abiding joy of being thankful.

If it ever starts to feel stale or mechanical, take a few days off and then come back to it, or try writing it at a different time of the day or sitting in a different place—this alone can stimulate your creativity.

Practising gratitude is a stepping stone towards creating a more positive bias in life, but it has to be *felt* in all your layers and not be a mental exercise only—move it out through your body and into your life. There is much more you can explore with a gratitude practice, using it to unpick old fixed ways of perceiving your life and yourself. For now, start simply but powerfully with these guidelines.

Chapter 12
Everyone Is Creative, Even You

Creativity is intelligence having fun.
~ Albert Einstein

You are a creative being, everyone is. I hear so many people say, "Oh, I'm not creative." I also hear about the same number of people say, "I used to be creative, but I don't do it anymore." Both groups of people have become cut off from their deepest layer. Every soul is creative but maybe we need to reframe what creativity is.

For a long time, I would casually assign the term creative only to artists. They sing, dance, write, make music and so on. That certainly is one expression of creativity. However, this sort of creativity has become transactional in our modern world. So many of the products of artistic creativity can be purchased by us, the consumers. They become commodities. We judge the output of an artist on whether we like what they created, and we give them money if we do. There's a transaction and the creative value is determined by the purchaser, rather than being inherent in the creative process itself.

True creativity isn't about creating a product for someone else to consume, although it can be for some people. True creativity is inherent within all of us. What you are creating is your *life*. Your life is like a novel or a screen play that no one has written yet. *You* get to craft your life. You wake up every morning and either intentionally create your day, or repeat yesterday out of habit, because you told yourself you are not creative, or you're too busy to be creative or you think you have no choice. All the joy got sucked out of the day and you gave away your power. Your power is in the remembrance that you are the author of your life story, not someone else.

You are a creator having fun, to paraphrase Einstein. Does that describe you? Do you recognise this as who you are, or do you identify with your doubts and excuses, the list of tasks your surface self must do? Your entire life is a work of art, not an eternal to-do list.

Another aspect of ananda and the entire universe of which you are but a drop, is abundance. We live in an expanding universe. Abundance means flow, but also fullness and richness, there is nothing lacking. It's you as that bright shiny silver ball before the dents appeared. There exists an infinite number of possibilities for how your day will flow, how your life will flow if you can become free from your habitual ways of thinking and doing life, free from your fears and limiting beliefs.

When you play a computer game, the game has already been programmed with every possible outcome for every possible move. The outcome you get depends on the move you select. You work the same way. The entire catalogue for how the next moment of your life will flow depends on the move you select in this moment, from the infinite catalogue of possibilities. Each time you decide to do something differently, rather than allowing your repetitive habits to decide for you, you are being creative. You are doing something new.

Your selection process lies in the next layer. You can either let habit choose or in the pause, before the habit kicks in, you have the opportunity to select another move and live that instead, just for today—you can go back to your habit again tomorrow if you want to.

I'll give you an example that I have played with. I can be quite judgemental, of myself, of others, of the world, and I don't like the feeling of judgement in my body—it makes me feel nauseous. So, I decided one day, just for that day, that I was going to lead with love (which is an ananda quality). Whatever comes my way I will pause, tap into the feeling of love within me (which feels so much more expansive and delicious than the nausea of judgement), and then I would respond from that place. Oh, my giddy aunt, the difference it made to my day was incredible.

I had an email from a client who wanted to stop working with me. Normally, this would have brought up fear, rejection, anxiety, and tension in me, activating my old wounds of not being good enough, as well as 'things have gone wrong and it's all my fault'. Instead of jumping straight into a reply, I paused and felt into her energy, her fears and connected lovingly with myself and with this client. I responded with understanding and wishing nothing but her highest good. She immediately replied with relief, confirmed she was just feeling scared that she would fail, and she remained as a client, ultimately getting to the place in her life where she wanted to be. This was just one way in that day that I opted out of my old, conditioned reactions, and crafted my day differently, to the benefit of myself and everyone I interacted with. I made a different selection. Creativity is to open up to a different possibility, interrupt a pattern, and see how it plays out.

Leading with love felt so good, that I now try to remember to set this intention every day. Sometimes I forget but the uncomfortable feeling of judgement (so long as I'm not too busy or too distracted to notice it) quickly reminds me that I am letting my old habits lead today. I much prefer inhabiting a body infused with the expansive feelings of love, than the contracted feeling of judgement, and it's much better for my health.

When we live from the inside out, we are in our power of choice, we are creators. When we forget our power we are left with only one option, which is to react to life coming at us, we are reactors. Both creator and reactor contain the same seven letters and you get to choose how you arrange them.

Layer 2 is where we begin to either block or channel the joy. So, if you want to be a creator of more love, joy, wonder, abundance, and power in your life, please read on.

Part 3

Habits and Memories – *Vijnana Maya Kosha*

Chapter 13
Embodied Wisdom

We don't receive wisdom; we must discover it for ourselves
After a journey that no one can take for us or spare us.
~ Marcel Proust

The name of the second layer is **Vijnana,** pronounced vee-yanna. It is defined as embodied or applied wisdom. If only we were wise!

In practice, this layer holds the programmed motivations and drivers that lead to your behaviours, through which you create your life. It is the filtering layer which either allows joy, love, and creativity to flow through you or stops it dead in its tracks.

If only all your filters directed the free, spontaneous outward flow of joy, your life would be amazing indeed, wouldn't it? But many of the deep unconscious filters have become blocked with old, accumulated content that is working against you.

Stephen Fry in his wonderful book *Mythos* introduces us to all the Greek gods and goddesses, bringing them up to date and relevant to the modern age. In there, we learn about the Goddess Mnemosyne (don't worry about pronouncing it!). At the start of the universe, when she was still young, she was considered a 'very shallow, silly and ignorant being, who knew nothing and appeared to understand less'. But she became so much more 'for each day that passed she got smarter and smarter' and 'as the years passed, her endless capacity for the storage of information and sensory experience would make her wiser than almost anyone'. She was the Goddess of Memory.

We record all our memories in this layer. It is the storehouse, like with Mnemosyne, of all information and sensory experiences, and it forms the bedrock of who we think we are—our historical biography. But we already know that we are more than our historical record, we are creative beings connected to infinite possibility.

This layer doesn't exist only in the brain. It is the alive autonomic (automatic) nervous system running through your entire physical body, touching every cell and vijnana is the repository, not only of memories, but of habit.

Every experience, but most especially, emotionally charged experiences, becomes stored here. Depending on what you store, you may become wise indeed, or just more and more wounded, stuck, and disgruntled. It will depend on whether those memories channel your joy, love and creativity or block it.

In an ideal situation, this layer provides you with a storehouse of learning: the wisdom of your past experiences, which you continue to apply in your life, in an effortless and automatic way, freeing your thinking mind up to learn new things. Ideally, this layer gives you the faith and trust to continue to explore, grow and experience more delight. As your wisdom bank grows your abilities in the world grow too. But what if the earliest memories and experiences you laid down, which became the very foundation of your life, were fearful, broken, and distorted, given to you by adults who were also fearful and broken?

Your 'wisdom' is what you accumulate, and you continue to create more of the same because it works automatically. Your wisdom bank can end up overloaded with fear and negativity.

Instead of interpreting vijnana as 'applied wisdom', we should perhaps read it as 'applied memories'. When this is left to run on automatic, you are doomed to keep repeating the memories you have acquired until you *decide* to acquire something *else*.

The second layer is the first filter which will either channel your power, joy, love, desires, and curiosity out into your life or like a dirty sieve, will block that flow, allowing only a portion of your greatness to come through, if any. It all depends on how dense the content of this layer is and how you continue to add to it.

This is the realm of the survival brain, the subconscious mind, and your habits—habits of belief and habits of behaviour. It contains useful things such as muscle memory, so you don't need to re-learn how to walk every morning and less useful things such as the belief 'I am not worthy to receive love', and every possible thing in between.

This part of your autonomic nervous system is about efficiency, and drives 95% of everything you do, without using the thinking mind at all. This should free up your thinking mind for learning new things, but this bundle of habits also determines your feelings and your vibration. The first layer, ananda, was about getting in touch with who you really are, what you love, and what you want at a soul level. The second layer is about how you *feel* about what you want, and it is dependent on all the stories you have created and made automatic around your past experiences.

Your soul may want to become one thing, but based on past experiences (memories), do you feel worthy of it? Do you feel capable? Do you believe you can be successful at bringing it into your life? Do you believe that you don't have time to pursue your passions? Do you believe your needs come last? And so on…

Many of these beliefs are just below your conscious awareness, lurking unseen in the swamp of your secret self—that part of you that you hide from others and even from yourself. By bringing your beliefs up into the light of your honest, non-judgemental awareness and getting to know them, you can bring about real change, and it's easier to do than you think. You just need to be willing to be with your feelings, which we'll get more into in the fourth layer. For now, know that you draw to you only the things which are a vibrational match to your vibration, your 'vibes' attract similar vibes and it all comes from the beliefs you hold about yourself. Your beliefs are rooted in the past—all your previous experiences and what other people have told you.

If you don't like what you are attracting into your life, then take the time to discover how you *really* feel about the things you *say* you want.

This layer doesn't really have words—those arise from the next layer. The subconscious mind communicates in pictures, feelings, and emotions, which is why using positive self-talk and even talk therapy will have only a limited effect if they don't change the feelings and vibrations of the body. Talk alone communicates with the thinking mind (the third layer), but not this one, and since this one governs almost everything you do, you need a way to understand what is in this layer if you want to live life differently.

To turn this layer from applied memories and habits to applied wisdom, you must go on an inner journey, a journey no one can take for you.

Chapter 14
Intuition

There is a voice that doesn't use words, listen.
~ Rumi

We use our ears to listen to the sounds around us but there is a voice, a deep knowing that is the voice of your soul. It doesn't use words because it has spoken for longer than language has existed. Young children, before they learn to speak, hear it, and respond to it without thinking and you can learn to reconnect with it too. It's intuition.

Intuition is that deep sense of knowing. It's a sense of knowing that you cannot explain. Its voice is quiet and gentle, easily drowned out by the noise of your chatterbox mind. Trying to hear it is like trying to hear a whisper in a nightclub. Intuition is felt.

Intuition is embodied wisdom. Intuition is how the vijnana layer helps the soul flow outwards in a positive way. When we are selecting what we want to do at this moment, intuition is the quiet voice arising from the soul, showing you the best next step to let joy continue its journey out and through you. It amplifies physical feelings of 'yes' and 'no' through pictures and feelings. When the soul says 'yes' to something it wants, that's like turning the key in the ignition of your car—things wake up, desire flows. The vijnana layer and your intuition are where you feel the vibration of the car, the potential and you see where you want to go next.

It is linked to action because embodied wisdom (vijnana) is *applied.* Following your intuition is the application—*doing* what your heart and soul know is the right next move for you. But the content of this layer is so cluttered with fear and noisy neurotic lies, that you no longer hear the quiet-spoken intuition. In the rare quiet moment when you do catch its gentle prompting, you pretend you didn't and get on with your habitual way of controlling and battling your way through life.

One of the great benefits of slowing down your life, and simplifying it, is that you experience more internal space. Simply by doing less, you receive more gaps between the content of your day. You know how beneficial it is to book a lunch break into your schedule, or fifteen minutes between appointments so that you can breathe and gather your wits. When you live a life choc-a-bloc full, you rush, you struggle to keep up, and you fall prey to your habits—habits of doing and habits of thinking, to get through the day on automatic, because anything automatic requires less energy—it has become efficient at doing what it has always done.

Constant busyness is the enemy of wisdom because you access intuition in the spaces, not in the content: the spaces between activities and the spaces between thoughts. It's why so many people take up meditation, in recognition that they have built a life without windows, no way for the light to come in. The space between thoughts lets the light in—*and* you let your light out. A life without spaces is a life that is completely dependent on habit, destined to constantly recreate the past over and over again, like a photocopier. Space brings more joy, creativity, and juice to your life.

Learning to distinguish the voice of intuition from my mind content and its associated fears took me until my fifties. I had been hearing that voice on and off all my life, sometimes I even acted on it, not knowing what it was, and always with the best results. There were times I could look back on and know that I overrode my intuition, and the results were awful. At those times, I would find myself lamenting, "If only I had listened to my instincts"...as I called it back then. Yet, I kept on overriding rather than trusting it.

I now recognise that my intuitive voice comes in first, usually as a picture, a feeling and a physical sensation, and my mind content arrives later, but louder. My intuitive voice is drama-free, clear, and grounded, and makes me feel expanded. Whereas my mind voice is fear-based, control-based and sounds a bit like an agitated teenager. It makes me feel contracted, especially around my gut.

For example, when trying to decide whether to close a community Facebook group I had started which had been irritating me (there's a clue there I chose to ignore for months!), I agonised for such a long time over the decision. I was trying to decide with my thinking mind instead of my intuition. Repetitive thoughts plagued me, such as there were people in the group who I wanted to connect with, I needed a platform to have a conversation with others, I had spent a lot of time building it (my personal favourite ball and chain, that one)…and so on…

In the end, I decided to sit quietly, breathe with it and ask myself the question: should I keep it open? Immediately my gut, just above my navel tightened and I felt a strong sense of 'no, it's time to let it go, it doesn't light you up anymore'. A split second later, the thoughts started forcing their way in…just give it another month, try some new content, blah, blah, blah. It would have been so easy to miss the immediate, slight tensing of my tummy and indeed, give it another month. But I have learned to trust that gut reaction because I know it's where I feel my intuition. Other people may feel it in the chest or other areas, but you will come to know where it lives in you. With a large helping of doubt, I closed the group. Hardly anyone noticed. It was totally the right thing to do and to think I could have gone on pushing, struggling, and getting even more frustrated if I had listened to my head.

How you get in touch with this voice is simple, it's been waiting for a long time to have a conversation with you. Give yourself permission for it to be easy but be patient, you're building a new relationship, so don't rush—get to know it, woo it. Get quiet and relaxed and become attentive. Then ask a question to which you know the answer is yes. You might ask, "Is my name ____?" Fill in the blank with whatever your name is. Watch for the instantaneous response in your body. You might feel something like more space, lightness, or a freeing of tension, even a picture—it can be so many things, get in touch with *your* yes.

Then ask a question that you know the answer is a strong no, such as, "Do I like Brussels sprouts (if like me, you don't)?" Notice where and how your body responds. Again, it can be a physical sensation like tension, it might be a sound inside you, an image or even an old memory. Get to know what *your* no response is.

Practise this for a while, with yes and no questions you know the answers to so you can really get to know and trust your intuitive answers. Be patient, your intuition may be shy. Then move on to the current questions you have about decisions you want to make now (frame them as yes/no questions). Be prepared for the answers to feel vague again. When we don't know the answer, our fear-based reactions jump in quickly to take control. Sometimes intuition comes through in words, like, "Ooh, no don't do that," and sometimes it can be deeply held fears that get activated from the survival brain which are hard to put into words. Be patient and willing to ask the question for many days until you feel the intuitive response become clearer. If you are anything like me, even as you put that decision into action, you can still experience doubt in that moment—that's okay. But watch what happens afterwards. Do you get confirmation that you did indeed make the right decision? Make a note of that, celebrate that and it will strengthen your trust in this quiet voice that always knows your best next move.

Practise responding to intuitive impulses as they arise in your day. If you get the urge to call someone, someone you may not have thought about in years, do it. Be curious and who knows where it might lead? You do not need to know why—the addiction to needing to know everything and to following your agenda is getting in your way. Actually, if you can understand it then it's not your intuition and this is why the thinking mind is scared—it likes to know. Stepping into the unknown is you being creative and curious and there is a sense of anticipation involved too. All great ananda qualities, so let the magic in.

You might be drawn to a book in the bookshop, and again you've no idea why, but follow the impulse and read it, keeping in mind that you were drawn to the book intuitively. Notice what really resonates with you. There are so many ways intuition shows up throughout every day.

Living in close contact with your intuition is what keeps you connected with your joy, curiosity, and creative power, ensuring this is what you are acting from instead of from the storehouse of old wounds and fears. Intuition guides you to feel what your next move is and helps you determine and clarify that what you desire is coming from your soul, your heart, and your centre. The vijnana layer is currently jammed full of unhelpful and untrue content, much of which you have accumulated from other people. This content is not wisdom and is blocking both your ability to hear your intuitive voice and the pursuit of what your soul came here to enjoy.

Chapter 15
Habits

The power of our beliefs can work in either direction to become life-affirming or life-denying.
~ Gregg Braden

We move from the joy layer through the habit layer, which is essentially the automatic operating system and software for this wonderful machine—your body-mind.

During the first ten years of your life, you were developing a sense of who you are, based on the experiences you were having during this time. There were dynamics going on around you, out of your control. What was programmed into you from the people and environment you found yourself in, were the emotionally impactful or repetitive experiences.

In fact, much of the sense of self you have and the beliefs you hold, are not yours at all but were embedded into you from the experiences and people you encountered, which they inherited from somebody else. You are not the events that happened to you, but they shaped who you *feel* you are—a sense of this is me, but that is not me.

Before you had any understanding of the spoken language that you have now, you spoke a clear and universal language—you were able, like all living things, to understand energy and instincts. If something didn't feel right to you, you pulled away and avoided it. If something felt safe, loving, or exciting you were drawn towards it. From a grounded sense of safety, you felt confident to venture out and explore. It was all instinctual because your entire body is a giant antenna system, sensing your environment and sending the information to your high-functioning nervous system.

Even the humble, single-celled amoeba does this—it is drawn towards nourishment and repulsed by poison. And you are far more complex than an amoeba. But do you trust this inner GPS? Chances are you were programmed in childhood to override your instincts in order to fit into adult social and cultural norms, essentially other people's expectations of what is 'acceptable'.

On the day you arrived, you were like a brand-new laptop, still set to its default factory settings, full of potential for how it can be used, but until programmed, utterly useless. First, you must install the software you will need for how you want to use this laptop. In your case, you had to download the software of how to be a thriving human being *where you landed in the world*, and you received this without question, from your environment.

In that first decade of life, you were wide open, downloading all the behaviours and norms of your immediate vicinity, without any ability to reject or accept them—the subconscious mind accepts it all, like a giant sponge. You subconsciously learned how to survive, stay safe and hopefully even thrive, in the time and place you appeared. The programming of someone born into poverty in Tudor London would have been very different from someone born into relative wealth in the late twentieth century.

You can see this perhaps in the generations of your own family. I bought my first mobile phone at age thirty. I still struggle with it and dread new updates and applications. Yet my son, born in the age of technology, even at a very young age, five or six, could pick up any mobile phone and get it to do what he wanted from it. I certainly didn't teach him; he simply absorbed the know-how of his time and place—his 'normal'.

Even if people are born at the same time and to similar circumstances, no one else has had the exact same experiences as you, so no one has the exact same software.

You took in everything that helped you function and stay safe. It was lodged in the survival brain, which is a part of your brain and body with one sole function—to keep you alive. It reacts quickly, running every new experience past the database of all past experiences and how you felt about them at the time they were stored. All done more quickly than you can formulate a thought.

The survival brain doesn't waste storage capacity lodging trivial things. It tends to store only the most emotionally charged and life-preserving memories. Before you had words, you could still store memories (we call them pre-verbal impressions) in your instincts, impulses, and reflexes. Most importantly—they were in your *body*, not your head. They were implanted in your body to make you ready to react when confronted with danger, without having a debate in your thinking mind over all the possible options—you'd be dead before you made a decision.

As a child, the world around you and the people in it were big, and you were small. You adopted some effective and novel protective behaviours to keep yourself physically, emotionally, and mentally safe *at the time*.

These protective behaviours never went away and instead became your core programmes—your deeply held beliefs. Beliefs are thoughts which you hold as truths about the world and about yourself. But beliefs are *not* necessarily true, they just *feel* like they are, especially if the associated feelings are powerful and uncomfortable.

It's worth emphasising here that safety was two-fold: one, it was about physically keeping you alive, and two, it was the safety to be *you* just as you are. Now in the twenty-first-century Western world, perhaps the most powerful role of the survival brain is the latter: is it safe to be authentically you?

Your early successful responses became habitual ways of making sense of your life and yourself, right into adulthood. Have you ever found yourself reacting to a situation, not from clear, adult reasoning but more like a toddler having a temper tantrum? When an old belief is prodded, you go straight back to the moment that belief was first stored, that age, and you react immediately, in the same way you learned to react back then. It worked then when you were three or four, after all, you're still here, aren't you? Now you're fifty or more, and there are better ways of getting your needs met but the habit is there—programmed in and activated before you can blink.

Survival mechanisms need to act immediately, there is no time to debate the various strategies available when you are confronted by a lion—survival kicks in, bypassing conscious thought. Every time an old wound is pressed, your survival mechanism reacts in the same way as meeting a predator—decisively. Have you ever reacted without thinking and later felt regretful and a bit ashamed? You had already flared up before you knew what you were doing, but that's normal for the survival brain. That part of you feels successful because you are still living—yay, we won! So, it will be ready next time too—it gets stronger with every activation.

Habits and reactions are a lot like a bobsleigh run. Once you start at the top, before you know it you are at the bottom, and the whole thing has run its course. There's no getting off halfway down simply because you've changed your mind. Once you step onto the ice, you're committed, and the result is a foregone conclusion—you find yourself at the bottom. That's how our deep programming works—when a habitual belief is set in motion (i.e., you step on the ice) it plays out to its guaranteed conclusion automatically.

Not all habits are bad of course—making something habitual means you don't have to think about routine things all the time. You also don't need to make the same decision repeatedly. This frees up so much brain space for other things—creative pursuits that are, by definition, not habitual because you are making something new, not simply repeating yesterday. Creativity is your soul's energy, and it wants an avenue to express itself, so habits that take care of daily life tasks help with that.

Does your life feel like 365 identical days, year after year? If so, it may be time for a habit upgrade. There is a difference between habits you adopt to survive and habits you choose in order to thrive. Survival is a different experience than *thrival* (my word). Survival is protection and thrival is growth. Survival is avoidance of pain, thrival is the pursuit of joy. Upgrade to habits and beliefs that automatically create thrival in your life and leave the survival instincts for when you really need them, like avoiding a collision on the motorway, rather than how you start every day.

It's a matter of examining your habits of thought, feeling and activity—make them conscious (using the next layer) and decide which ones serve you and which don't. Then set about re-programming what you do want. Ideally, you want to embed everyday behaviours which lift you up, support the life you want to create and amplify the free flow of joy, love, curiosity, and creativity into your daily life. You want these to be as automated as possible. You also want habits which support your positivity bias to run automatically. New habits are embedded the same way as the ones you already have—through repetition and with positive emotion.

Decide how you want to use your precious resources of time and energy to create your best life. Decide what feelings and attitudes you want to inhabit, even during the most mundane moments of your life. Good habits make creativity and joy easy; confining and outdated habits stifle it.

Let's consider some examples of beliefs:

Say in your early life, you were told repeatedly that you weren't good enough, constantly being told off for falling short of the expectations of others. For some reason, the adults around you forgot that you were a small child learning to navigate the complexity of a physical and emotional body and they expected you to just know how it worked and behave the same as a fully grown adult would. (To be honest, I haven't met that many fully grown adults who are skilful at expressing their emotions effectively, so why we think a small child would be able to, is beyond me).

You heard this so often, that for you, 'you are not good enough' became a 'truth'—I am not good enough. As you grew up, you didn't need the adults around you to say this to you anymore—you were more than able to say it to yourself and 'know' it to be true. It's not true at all, it's just a thought, someone else's wonky belief, repeated so often that you came to believe it as well. It's a small, wounded part of you but you are building your life on this foundation.

As an adult, you may no longer hear those words inside you anymore. It has become so familiar that you become desensitised to it. Just like if you walk into a room and notice the scent clearly, but after half an hour you are no longer aware of it. The story, the programme is still there running, but it's unseen and anything that clicks on the 'I'm not good enough' button, activates the wound and the emotional need that wasn't met when you were young. Each time the button is pressed it elicits a predictable response, which flows out into your body and confirms to your sense of self, "You see—this *is* true, I am not good enough," and you believe it even more. You miss the promotion, you don't get the job you applied for, your relationships never work out...all because good things happening in your life don't align with your inner sense of self. You're running on a programme that says, "I'm not good enough," so of course you are not going to have a great new job—because that's not a match with the energy you are emitting. Your sense of identity will reject, push away, sabotage, and ignore anything which doesn't confirm its story.

Your sense of identity (also referred to as your ego or self-image) is a collection of all your beliefs, all the stories you have adopted from the events you have experienced in your life and the meaning you attached to them. They all live in the second layer—the subconscious layer, the habit layer and your sense of identity is directing 95% of what you do and most of the time you are completely unaware of it.

Just as you can't see the electricity powering the light when you turn on the light switch, you just see the light come on and ignore the science of how electricity works; so too you don't see your programmes, you only see the result of them—look around at your life right now and you will see the sum total of all your programmes. Your inner self-identity shows up as your outer life.

The good news is that you can install an upgrade, just as you do periodically in your laptop or phone. You install your new programmes and habits the same way your original programmes got in there, only this time *you* get to decide what your beliefs and habits will be, rather than someone else, passing on their faulty programming to you.

In his book *Psycho-cybernetics* (don't be put off by the title—it's a great book and an easy read), Maxwell Maltz coined the term your 'Self-Image'. It's the full collection of your programmed beliefs and habits, your sense of identity and how you feel. If someone asks you, "Who are you?" you might answer:

Well, I am a woman in my fifties, I am British, white, five feet three, I love reading, exploring and yoga. That's me in a nutshell but of course, like everyone, I am more than this short sentence can convey.

You are also an inventory of your limiting beliefs, things like I am not worthy of nice things, my needs come last, I have to do everything perfectly because otherwise, I get into trouble, I feel like an imposter most of the time, when things go wrong it's always my fault, I can never earn more than £x a year because of___ (fill in your own excuse) and so on.

Just to be balanced though, there will be some life-affirming beliefs in there too: I am not a quitter, I keep going until something is complete, I am a caring person, I love to help others, etc. In fact, a healthy sense of self allows you to simultaneously own your skills and talents with confidence and be humble around your challenges. We are all a mixture of both and a work in progress. Our challenges present us with an edge, the edge of what doesn't feel easy for us. This edge is a barrier we can lean into, explore, and expand into so that we can become more, grow and thrive. We need to learn to be at ease with the duality of what's easy and what's an edge for us; what expands and what contracts us; what lights us up and what darkens us. If you are willing to be with it, rather than rush to fix or suppress it, then every sticky and uncomfortable part of yourself is an invitation to create something else, something brand-new, and *creating* establishes you back in your joy layer, closer to your soul.

It can take years to unearth all your skulking beliefs, but they do reveal themselves one by one if you stay curious and want to keep growing. It can be easier to discover what your hidden beliefs are by looking outward—at the life you have created, especially life patterns which show up over and over.

Take a quick inventory of your outer world:
On a scale of 1–10, with 1 being rock-bottom and 10 being magnificent, rate the following areas of your life:

- Your primary relationship
  1 2 3 4 5 6 7 8 9 10
- Other close relationships (you can do a separate score for each person)
  1 2 3 4 5 6 7 8 9 10
- Social life
  1 2 3 4 5 6 7 8 9 10
- Financial health, i.e., wealth abundance
  1 2 3 4 5 6 7 8 9 10
- Physical health
  1 2 3 4 5 6 7 8 9 10
- Mental health, i.e., flexibility to go with life's ups and downs
  1 2 3 4 5 6 7 8 9 10
- Home environment
  1 2 3 4 5 6 7 8 9 10
- Career satisfaction and fulfilment
  1 2 3 4 5 6 7 8 9 10

Then, pick just two areas—one you feel is doing well (your highest score) and one not so well (scored low), and I encourage you to go back and do this for each category when you have the time.

We will start with the positive first. Pick the category where you scored the highest, if there's more than one with the same score, simply choose whichever one you are most drawn to.

Write out in your journal everything going on in this category. Suppose you chose '*home environment*'. Describe your home environment as fully as you can.

For example:

I love my home and spending time there. It is my haven from the crazy world and the busyness of work. It's warm and bright, with a log burner in the living room. I love curling up by the fire in the evenings, reading a book and enjoying a glass of wine. The whole family comes together in the home, and we spend our evening meals chatting and cooking together.

I have a nice big bedroom with a large wardrobe for my gorgeous clothes and shoes. The bathroom is tranquil, and I enjoy soaking in the bath on a Sunday morning whilst everyone else is still asleep.

I have a small garden, which is okay because it's easy to look after. It has some pots for colour, a row of runner beans and a bistro table and chairs for catching the sun with a cup of tea.

You get the idea—this may not be your reality, in fact, it's not mine either!

Once you have written it out, read it back, close your eyes and *feel* the sensations in your body. As you visualise your home and all that you love about it, notice your body starting to respond as if you are there, experiencing it right now. You may notice a change in your breath, your temperature, shifting tensions either coming or going and so on.

The subconscious mind loves a story but has no concept of the past or future—everything is happening *now*. Every time you let your mind drift to what you love, real or imagined, you allow the joy layer to percolate into the present moment, your subconscious mind believes it's happening right now. Your nervous system starts to communicate to every cell in your body that life is good, you are safe, you are content and it's safe to relax. Your body expresses good feelings.

Visualisation is a powerful mental faculty that takes some practice to develop for most people. Learning to see and hold a picture in your mind's eye is an accessible way into meditation for many people, especially if you listen to a guided visualisation to stop the mind from wandering.

Once you can see it, the most important step is to *feel* the body's response to the picture, and this can certainly seem challenging at the beginning. It's helpful to develop this skill under the guidance of a coach because feeling, not thinking, is where the power is. You want an embodied awareness of joy, discovering where joy lives in your body.

Everything which occurs in the layer of the subconscious mind flows outward and is experienced in the body, so becoming more in tune with your *body* is essential for unpicking old stories and programming in the new ones. It's not enough to just think positive thoughts, you must feel them. Otherwise, positive thinking is just like putting icing on a cowpat—it looks nice on the surface but underneath it's still a cowpat.

You cannot know joy without a body to experience joy, similarly for love and anger—it all plays out in the theatre of the body and here's the best bit—only you get to experience it your way because no one else lives inside you.

Now let's explore a less satisfying category. Use your intuition here—if you have one category that scores, say 1, exploring that might really trigger strong feelings in you, connected to deep wounds and painful stories. If this is the case, leave that one to return to later and pick a category that was low but not your lowest score.

Now, in the same way as before, write out in your journal everything going on in this category. Suppose you chose '*financial health*'. Describe your financial situation as fully, and with as much detail as you can. Include emotions and frustrations too. Let it be as long and ranting as it needs to be to get everything out.

For example:

I never have enough money. Every month I go further into the red and I can't see how this is going to ever improve. I asked for a pay rise and it got turned down. I have always struggled with money and never had enough. Last year I got my purse stolen and it had £100 in it. Things like this always seem to happen to me. I see everyone else around me buying whatever they want, it seems, but I can't...

You get the picture!

Just as before, once you have written it out, read it back, close your eyes and feel into the body.

How easy was it to get into your story with the less satisfying category?

How did your body change? Maybe you felt your chest slump forward and down or maybe your jaw clenched, and your breathing got quicker and shallower.

All these changes in your body (the nice and the not-so-nice) occurred just because of two stories you chose to play on the screen of your mind. Your deep subconscious thoughts do not live just in your brain, the entire body participates. Can you start to see how your thoughts and feelings might be leading to the tension you feel in your muscles? The headaches? The IBS? The immune problems? The fatigue?

When you thought of the category that was not as satisfying, how quickly did the supporting stories show up? Negative stories come as a box set—it starts as one and is quickly followed by the stories of justification, past hurts, who's to blame and why your life is always going to be like this. We all love drama, it seems.

But to go back to the bobsleigh analogy—once you jump onto the negativity ice you are at the bottom before you know it—mired in feelings of misery, frustration, blame, tension, gripping and victimhood—boom! I bet you've already forgotten the first category you visualised and yet, at the time, you were fully immersed in what was great in your life. Now you've crashed your bobsleigh into the pit of pissed-off-ness and you feel stuck there.

But rewind. There was a brief moment, easy to miss, where you made a choice, even if it felt as if someone else was making the choice for you, they weren't. Your programming kicked in super-fast but there was a space between the trigger (listening to your own story) and the result—flying down the habitual, reactive pattern and feeling dissatisfied. In that space, you could have decided to *not step onto the ice*.

It requires great self-awareness but like any skill, it can be developed with practice. It's one of the key benefits of practices like meditation, breathwork and yoga—all these train us to expand that pause and be *with* a thought or feeling, noticing our habitual impulses without reacting to them, rushing to push them away or change them. What we can be with, we can transcend and release. In the remaining space, we can choose differently and programme in new responses. It all begins with *allowing* discomfort to be truly felt but without reacting.

You came into this world as a joyful, creative, and curious soul, with a body and mind to enable you to feel the fullness of life and to carry you wherever you wanted to go. Reclaim that soul, and you can start to steer your life again and loosen the stranglehold that your old programming has over you.

As you practise being more present with sensations rather than reacting to them blindly, the pauses at the top of the bobsleigh run expand. You have time to see that you have been triggered but like a slow-motion scene in a movie you can say, "Not this time buddy, I am not getting on the ice today." Sometimes your reactions will catch you and there you are at the bottom, on your bum wondering how you got there. Never mind. Forget about blame and self-criticism, these are old, faulty programmes which aren't helpful. Pick yourself up, come back to now, and be ready for the next opportunity to practise your new way. The idea is not to be perfect at this. We live in a culture which glorifies perfection and the finished product. Instead, be willing to be in the process of becoming, rather than at the end of the process. It's all in the repetition.

All habits work the same way. Making the same unconscious choice repeatedly brings the same results, a feeling of certainty and dependability. This is a good thing if you like the results. But if you don't then it's time for new choices, repeated, which will bring different results and then watch your life change beyond your wildest dreams. Never underestimate the creative power of a different choice.

> The next step is to go back to the category you chose first—the one that felt satisfying and make a list of all your behaviours, thoughts and feelings that contribute to your satisfaction in this area.
>
> Let me be really clear here, list only the things that *you* do, think, feel and believe because it's not your job to change anyone else—that's their path. You only get to work on *you*.
>
> *Using the same example, you might list:*
>
> - *I regularly keep my home clean and well-lit.*
> - *When I walk through the door, I take off my worries with my coat.*
> - *I make sure I have half an hour alone to decompress before jumping in to make dinner or talk to the family.*
> - *I have a ritual around lighting the fire after dinner and sitting by it without turning on the TV.*
> - *I set my alarm early on Sundays to make sure I get to soak in the bath before anyone else is awake.*
> - *We purposefully bought a home with a low-maintenance garden because I don't have the time or inclination to mow a lawn.*
> - *Every time I am home, and the sun is shining, I sit outside and take a pause with a cuppa.*

Hopefully, you get the idea—these are all things you are doing, that you are deciding are important to you, which are creating the happy and satisfied feeling you have in this category of your life. This is an example of where you are letting ananda through—you follow what you love, and it brings fulfilment and joy. Cleaning the bathroom may not be the most exciting experience, but creating a spotless house brings context and meaning to these everyday chores.

So next time you are on a downer and beating yourself up about all the things you are doing wrong, read this list. Look at all the things you are doing right, all the success. Switch that positivity bias back onto the high setting.

Be curious (first layer) rather than critical about how easily you slip into negative self-talk and how it feels in the body. Laugh at it and turn it around. Every time you can do this you are strengthening this ability just like all the repetitions in the gym are strengthening your biceps. Eventually, you can notice the very first stirring of a negative feeling, the old story that wants to jump in and take over, and you can quickly shift the feeling before it escalates. Essentially, in that moment of noticing, you are saying, "No, I am not getting onto the ice today."

Now go back to the unfavourable scenario where things were not going so well and do the same thing. Make a list of all your behaviours, thoughts, beliefs and feelings that contribute to your dissatisfaction.

Once again, only list the things that *you* do, think, and feel because it's not your job to change anyone else—that's their path. However much you want to put the blame on someone or something outside of you (your boss, the economy, your job, COVID, etc), you only get to work on yourself. Your outer life only shifts once the inner stance has shifted…we all get this the wrong way around.

Using the same example, you might list:

- *I don't budget or track my spending so I don't actually know where my money goes.*
- *I say to myself that I will save whatever I have left at the end of the month and I never have anything left…but I don't track it, so I don't know where it goes.*
- *I can't resist buying new clothes when I go shopping on Saturdays.*
- *I deserve a treat, like a new handbag after a tough week.*
- *I have a deep belief that I can't earn more than I do, I never have and I never will (spoiler alert: you can).*
- *I believe my income is in the hands of my employer (spoiler alert: it's not).*
- *I am scared to change my job.*
- *I believe being rich means you're a bad person (spoiler alert: this one means your subconscious mind is going to protect you from ever being labelled a 'bad person' by never letting you have money!)*

And so on…Don't skimp on this section—there are some gems to mine here and you may just discover some deep beliefs that you were completely unaware of.

Can you see some habitual things you are doing, or avoiding doing, that are keeping you stuck where you are? In the example above, not tracking your spending means you are always left in the dark about where your money goes, so trying to economise will be pointless and built upon ignorance. You cannot build a budget that enables you to save if you don't really know where your money is going. This is a new habit you can choose to put into practice.

The same might be true for losing weight or trying to adopt a diet that promotes better health. If I had a pound for every person I have spoken to about their diet who told me, "Well, I try to eat a healthy diet," I would be a millionaire. When I dig deeper and ask what they ate yesterday, there are a lot of unhelpful foods on the list, if their goal is to lose weight or get healthy. Tracking creates clarity, truth and ownership. It's not about assigning blame but getting really clear. Make what is unconscious (unseen) seen, so you can do something with that information. If the thought of tracking brings up uncomfortable feelings, then there's a belief in there that needs to also be addressed.

Armed with a truthful report of what is happening you can now switch to what you want to happen…more on that in a moment.

As well as the things you are doing (or not doing) you'll notice there will be beliefs on your list that you live by in this unsatisfactory situation. For example, "I have a belief that I can't earn more than I do, it's not in my hands" and it will be quickly followed by lots of examples and reasons to support this belief, based on the past, none of which are true in the future.

Whatever beliefs you listed, take a good look at each one and in a different colour, if you like, write down next to each one, who or where you got this belief from. Perhaps you heard your parents say it repeatedly about themselves as you were growing up…things like 'Money doesn't grow on trees' and other statements implying that money was a limited resource and there was not enough, they weren't lucky enough to have it, only other people had that sort of luck and so on.

We live in an abundant, creative, and expanding universe, our economies are always trying to 'grow'. Countries, businesses, and people all strive to increase not just wealth, but all forms of abundance and some do it very successfully. But the implication of our collective agreement that resources are scarce, is that if someone's wealth is going up, then it's because someone else's is going down (because there is only a limited amount to go around). One person gets more at the expense of someone else. Just look at the words 'At the expense of'—collective, shared beliefs are hidden in plain view in our everyday language.

At the level of ananda, you tap into the truth that you exist in abundance; the content of your belief layer may tell you the opposite. Now you have an internal battle going on. Beliefs can change because they are not real.

Thoughts are just internalised language, a conversation you have with yourself, playing both sides of the dialogue. Repeating these habitual thoughts keeps you stuck in the 'same old, same old'. When we shift our perspective to remember that we live in an abundant and ever-expanding universe, we can see money as energy, a flow not a thing; that money is limitless. Rest in the inherent truth of who you *really* are, even as you allow and befriend the wounded parts of you that fear scarcity.

As you go back and look at the area in your life which scored low, ask yourself: what beliefs and habits can I adopt that would support what I want? What would allow joy, love and my heart's desire to flow into my life? This is a wish list, so don't edit out anything you feel won't ever happen or that you feel you are unworthy of (these are the very faulty beliefs we want to move on from!) This is an exercise in using your most powerful mental faculty, linked to your creativity—your imagination.

As Einstein said: *Whatever man can conceive, he can achieve*. Everything is made twice in this world—first in your mind's eye which creates the blueprint, then in physical reality. You decide you want a cup of tea, you picture it (however briefly), feel the desire for it (maybe as a feeling of thirst or a simple want) and then you get up, go to the kitchen, gather the ingredients and voila—you made a cup of tea appear in your reality for you to enjoy. See how it all comes back to deciding what you want, getting into action, trusting that it's on its way and then feeling the joy when it shows up?

Everything comes to life this way, even the things you think you don't want, like financial struggle or ill health. The creative life force doesn't understand labels like good or bad—everything just is what it is. This book began as a desire in me, I saw and felt all the content and even pictured the front cover in my mind. I got to work, battled my doubts and insecurities, uncovered the limiting beliefs that were creating resistance in me, procrastinated for ages, stayed in touch with the deep desire to create it and here it is. After what felt like a year of wrestling a bear, finally from existing only in my imagination, you are now able to hold it in your hands and share something that began privately inside my heart.

Most people have the creation process the wrong way around. You hear people say things like, 'When I win the lottery then I'll be happy' or 'When all the stress at work dies down, then I can start taking better care of myself'. No. As Neville Goddard says in his many books—start at the end. What do you want? When you have that—who will you be, how will you feel, what beliefs does that version of you have, what habits does she have? Start showing up as that version of yourself today with her habits. Start being happy by choice and you will feel as if you have already succeeded.

Let's have a go at creating change.

> For the category above that was less than satisfactory, write out the scenario as you would like it to be. Go into as much detail as possible—what are you doing, how are you feeling, who are you interacting with, even what you're wearing and so on?
>
> Really flesh it out. Also, write it in the present tense as if it's happening now—because the subconscious mind only understands now, not the future—you don't want to live in an eternal state of grasping for something. You want to be in the energy of completion.
>
> *For example:*
>
> *I have always got more than enough money for my needs. I track everything I have spent each day and it takes no longer than two minutes. I am empowered by this habit because I always know where I am financially. I easily adjust where I can see I am spending on things that aren't lighting me up or aren't necessary. At the start of each month, I save 10% of my pay straight away and my savings are growing month by month. I know I have enough to cover unexpected and unbudgeted expenses, and this means I can relax and not worry. I budget for the month ahead, adjusting for special occasions like birthdays and I always stick to what I planned because I choose to live in integrity with my desire to be financially comfortable. I know I am worth more than my current salary and I am actively pursuing a new position which will be at least 20% more than I am earning now...*
>
> You get the picture.

I know exactly what you're thinking—well, that all sounds great, but I don't believe it will happen to me! I was there too!

Remember how your current beliefs got lodged in you? You heard, felt, and experienced them a lot over your early years. They may have come with an emotional impact too. Being yelled at was scary as a child and fear is a huge emotion, one of the biggest. Your survival brain saved and stored the most emotionally impactful memories because they were perceived by your small self as life-threatening. As an adult it's easy to say, it wasn't that bad, I know they didn't mean to scare me. But your survival brain was programmed when you were four or five and the fear then was real. One of the most nonsensical expressions I remember growing up was 'Sticks and stones can break my bones, but words can never hurt me'—it's utter nonsense. Bones mend quickly in comparison with emotional wounds. These emotional wounds are still activating the same protective behaviours today as the four-year-old version of yourself who still lives inside you.

So, we replace these old beliefs with new beliefs in the same way—through repetition and with as much positive emotion as we can experience around the vision we see for ourselves.

When I decided I wanted to write this book, I was terrified and felt really vulnerable, almost reverting to the shy five-year-old I used to be. I kept trying to ignore the way the book kept prompting me whenever my guard was down. The feeling of imposter syndrome is one of my protectors which comes up to try to keep me in my comfort zone (my safe zone). But I know that I am here to grow, as we all are. I also knew that the desire to write this particular book, in this particular way, was given to me and no one else, so that must mean I have everything I need to write it.

But still, I resisted. My logical brain could rationalise that I could do this, but the fears and stories aren't in the logical brain. I don't know as much as other people, and I don't think people will like the book, all these beliefs, and more came surging up! So, I set about working to replace these beliefs first—until I realised that this was another protective behaviour showing its face—procrastination in disguise! I was doing the inner work (which was necessary) but doing it to avoid the outer work of writing the actual book.

So, I made a deal with myself that I would work on the beliefs *as* I was writing the book. I wrote out the scenario that I wanted, which was to have written an impactful international bestseller that goes viral. Did I believe it at first? Hell no! I hoped it would be that, but a much bigger part of me experienced doubt. I wrote out what I was doing, where I was living, what I wore, where I went on holiday—everything I was doing now that I was an international bestselling author. The picture kept growing. I added in giving book talks, attending book signings, being interviewed…and scariest of all I decided that this version of me would be interviewed by Oprah. There was a lot of detail, but I started to feel she was me and I was her—we were one and the same and I started to get excited about the prospect of this all coming true. Excitement connected me to my soul rather than my fears and enabled me to get into action.

Thinking is not enough as you'll see when we get to the next layer. To make things change you must feel as if you have already accomplished it; that you have already grown. That feeling has a vibration that resonates with the end state of success. Where I was at the start of writing, was in the lower vibration of fear and doubt—that only resonates with failure, selling a couple of hundred copies and falling into obscurity—something I felt was absolutely going to be the result. Yuck, I didn't want to attract that! So, of course, I wouldn't allow myself to begin. If I never start, I can never fail, right?

I had to believe the opposite result (I am an international bestselling author of a book that went viral) even more strongly than I believed in failure…otherwise the failure energy was going to dominate.

Your final task, now that you have written out what you do want is exactly what I did too. You must repeat it ad nauseam every single day and start to picture it in your mind. You can add more details to the words as you see them in your mind's eye. The most important part is to *feel* it accomplished.

How would I feel when I had an international bestseller on the shelves of every bookstore I walked into? Flipping amazing I reckon! Confident, joyous, that, 'It's done, and it was easy' feeling, accomplished, grateful and so many other powerful feelings.

So, I wrote it out every day and read it out loud (your subconscious really loves to hear your own words in your own voice). I recorded it on a loop on my phone so I could listen to it in the car or in the bath, or at night when I couldn't sleep. I started cultivating the feelings I would have at the end, living as if I was already there. I started putting in my gratitude journal how grateful I was that my book had gone viral and was reaching thousands of people. I was grateful for the emails from happy readers. I started dressing a little differently—clothes that made me feel confident, the clothes that in my head, a bestselling author might wear and so on. I created the feeling before I created the book. And even as this goes to publication, I know in my heart that it is an international bestseller. It's just a matter of time for the outside world to catch up.

Repetition with feeling is the key. Start small, don't try to change every habit and belief at once. Pick just one or two and work to embody those, until they feel automatic. My two were: I did a daily breathwork practice to shift me to a higher energy, more confident state and I sat down to write with the belief that this was fun and easy.

Oh, did I hear you say, "Blimey that's a lot of work, not sure I can be bothered with all that?" Then I challenge you to find something else to pursue. Because, if getting to a place of being financially free, in a great relationship, travelling the world, whatever you want more of, doesn't light you up enough to get you into action, it's not what you really want, it's what you think you should want. Go back to layer 1 and ask yourself the questions again:

- What brings you joy?
- What do you love to do?
- What makes you feel alive and truly you?
- What would you do if money was no object, and you knew you couldn't fail?

The answer might terrify and excite you in equal measure. If it does, then I would suggest you have landed on the right thing for you. It's in your heart, not mine nor anyone else's. The universe is saying this path is available to you if you want to pursue it…so the question is, do you want to pursue it or let your old programmes keep you exactly where you are?

Part 4
The Thinking Mind –
Mano Maya Kosha

Chapter 16
You Got Stuck in Your Head

Do not use the mind to overcome by force,
you must fit into the ancient grooves naturally.
~ Hermit of Lotus Flower Peak

We arrive now at the third layer—the conscious mind and oh boy, this is where so many of our problems lie, but before we jump into that, let's explore how this layer is designed to help you create the life you want.

As the soul's delight expands outward, accompanied by your intuition, the beliefs and habits ideally support it: 'I can do this', 'I deserve all I desire', 'What I want wants me to pursue it', 'This is my purpose'. You have also acquired lots of useful life experience, stored in your memory bank so you can move more freely through life automatically. Your embodied wisdom layer should enable you to express yourself freely and authentically in all you want to do, through habits that are aligned with who you want to be in the world. In summary, the wisdom layer should amplify the joy layer and help bring it to life.

Having several options at your fingertips around what you want to pursue, you *make a decision*. You pick the one thing you want to explore and create next—the one that elicits a full-body yes. This is the final job of the embodied wisdom layer—to decide. Unfortunately, due to our wisdom layer being cluttered with limiting beliefs and doubts, most of us are trying to make all our decisions from the thinking mind, using logic instead of feeling. We go round in circles of repetitive thought tinged with anxiety, when in fact, the body is where we decide what is or is not for us.

Having decided to pursue something new, you may not know how to do it. There may be some gaps in your knowledge, experience, and skill set. You set about learning what you need to learn to bring your desire to creative fruition. This is the function of the thinking mind—*to learn new things*, not to make a decision about what you want. Let the body simply follow its true soul preferences and put the mind to work learning and mastering *how* to do it. Once you've learned what you need to, you make it automatic—it becomes a habit, embedded in the subconscious.

The need to learn new things means you don't know something and that's alright because you can learn the things you need. (Many people allow the lack of know-how to stop them in their tracks if they have false beliefs about their capacity to learn new things, their cleverness, how successful they were at school and so on, all of which are based on the past). Not knowing is a good thing, because your soul wants to explore the unknown, so not knowing means you're about to grow. The trouble comes when you forget this, and the unknown becomes a place to fear. You get busy thinking about your life, constantly agonising over all the 'what ifs?' rather than simply living your life, moment to moment, trusting that each next step will arrive one by one. Spontaneity and improvisation present a fearful place to the thinking mind which wants a complete, drafted life script, but spontaneity and improvisation are the pure energy of ananda; so there's an inner conflict. In so many of us, the thinking mind gets stuck in control mode, like an inner manager and the soul's needs get ignored. As a result, you shut down learning new things and keep repeating the old things, focussing on keeping life predictable and safe instead. When the thinking mind is at odds with the soul, it keeps you stuck in survival/protection mode.

We live in a wonderful and enticing world, with so many pulls on our attention, so many interesting and pleasurable opportunities dangled in front of our flitting, fickle minds every moment of every day, made worse by our constant addiction to the internet. These pulls on our attention threaten to distract us from what we have set our heart on, our chosen thing. This brings us to the next function of the thinking mind—*to provide focus and concentration* so that we can see the creative process through to the end; so, we can feel the satisfaction, gratitude, and delight of fulfilment. You know that feeling, I'm sure. It's like when you decide to spring clean the kitchen. So many more interesting things threaten to distract you, halfway through you wish you hadn't started but you keep going, stay on task, and then there is that lovely feeling of virtuous satisfaction at the end of it. You flop on the sofa feeling good about what you achieved and ready to relax. Imagine living every day like that—always ending the day feeling complete. You met the challenge, you succeeded! By definition then, you are successful and capable and that's a really empowering place to rest in. You have circled back to the experience of your own power, an ananda quality. It's certainly a better feeling than the low-grade stress of trying (and often failing) to *manage* your life for seventy-five years.

When applied according to its purpose, the thinking mind, like the embodied wisdom layer, helps you to bring your soul to life and materialise more of what lights up your heart. Just for a few breaths, imagine what the world would be like if we all brought more of our souls into the world. There would be more love, joy, peace, connection, tolerance, and self-belief. In my heart, that's a world worth working for. It starts with each of us individually. When you commit to living this way, you give permission to everyone you encounter to live this way too, without having to say a word. So many of us are living our lives the way we think other people want us to live them and what's the result? War, misery, hunger, depression, anxiety, chronic ill health…the list is endless. Maybe we should harness our thinking minds to our hearts instead of living exclusively from our heads and maybe, just maybe, we can create a whole new world. A big ask? Yes, but the only person you have any ability to change and evolve is you…so how about making yourself a creative project by choosing to bring more of your heart into everything you do, and less of your conditioning, fear, and control.

The third layer, the conscious mind, sits right in the middle, a transition from the soul and the illusive inner realms on the one side, and the tangible, outside world of form on the other. The thinking mind likes to compartmentalise and put things in separate boxes. As a result, this layer can create an illusion of separation between inner and outer experience—the mind-body split, even though we now know that 'mind' is in every cell of the body. We see ourselves as a collection of separate parts, rather than one integrated being. We try to fix or reject the parts, rather than looking for ways to feel more integrated, more whole.

Not only do we see ourselves as made up of separate parts, but we also see ourselves as separate from one another and from the planet and the universe we exist in, we don't see ourselves as an integral part of that jigsaw. Unlike the thinking mind, the heart and soul see everything as one continuum, forever interconnected. Where the mind sees a collection of a thousand random jigsaw pieces, the heart sees how they fit together to create one complete picture. Fed by our deeper fears, in this layer, we move from seeing what unites us, to what divides us, and the division further amplifies our feelings of not being safe. When we feel unsafe, we automatically adopt protective behaviours programmed into us from our past, to create the illusion of safety, without needing to think about it. Continually playing out our history keeps us from ever creating a bright new future. You only need to watch the news to see the effects of humanity living in its collective head.

When we get stuck in our heads, letting old wounds and fears drive our behaviour, life has the potential to become a constant battle for scarce resources (time, money, water, food, power, choice) instead of sharing and expanding joy, love, and connection. The soul knows that we live in an expanding and abundant universe, but the head doesn't—it just sees life in small pieces and wants to control them all.

In today's increasingly complex world, with a mind-boggling amount of sensory input, many people have become stuck here, living out their entire lives from just this layer. They forget that they have a soul and intuition that will never direct them off-course, and they have become increasingly disconnected and dissociated from the information and wisdom of the body.

The result is to exist entirely in the head, thinking about your life rather than truly experiencing it; trying to control all the outcomes. It's a life of rigidity and stress. If you are lucky, like I was, your body lets you down and you finally pay attention. You agree to slow down, simplify, learn to step out of control mode and start to *feel* again. I can honestly say I am glad I got Hashimoto's disease and two frozen shoulders because if I hadn't, I would still be letting my mind force me into the life it thinks I should be living, rather than flowing gracefully through the life my soul was meant to experience.

Living exclusively in our head, cut off from the soul and cut off from the wisdom of the body is the first problem with the thinking mind layer. The second problem comes down to the actual content of this layer—literally, the thoughts filling your mind and stopping you from being able to harness this amazing tool for growth. When the thinking mind isn't put to its intended purpose, it goes rogue. Let's dive into that in the next chapter.

Chapter 17
Has Your Mind Gone Feral?

Quiet the mind, and the soul will speak.
~ Ma Jaya Sati Bhagavati

The thinking mind is there to drive the pursuit of what you want by helping you to learn the skills you need, to support (not make) your decisions, and help you get there by the easiest route. As you learn new things and make them automatic, you grow. That's pretty much it. The thinking mind is not supposed to run your life, that's the job of the soul.

The Enlightenment, also known as the 'Age of Reason' has so much to answer for when it comes to our modern woes. In eighteenth-century Europe, the explosion of science, philosophy and politics, emphasised *reason*. Not a bad quality in and of itself, but it has led us into a culture of trying to think ourselves out of every predicament. We now find ourselves needing to 'figure out' how to do life. We have forgotten that we are an integral part of nature and there is a creative intelligence in the natural unfolding of every day, an intelligence which grew you from a single cell. Disconnected from nature, we no longer trust it. It's safe to let go of the need to have to figure everything out logically. The feeling of safety is something we receive from our body and its wisdom, not our thoughts. The more disconnected we are from the body, the more we rely on the thinking mind to engineer safety, and it's not what the thinking mind is for. It's as helpful as asking your dentist to fix your car.

Now, there is a place for using the mind, watching your thoughts, and choosing different ones, so that you can have a different outcome. It's called top-down regulation—using the mind to help widen your perspective, see hidden patterns, and shift your feelings. But on its own, top-down regulation is less than half the solution. Bottom-up regulation is much more effective because it's the information coming from your body that tells the survival brain whether it feels safe—physically and emotionally. All too often, we use the mind to try to force something to which the body is saying a big fat 'no'.

The over-reliance on the mind to drive and control our lives has rendered many of us slaves to our thoughts. They keep us awake at night, we go round and round in circles of worry, anxiety, and confusion.

The problem is further compounded by the level of complexity of modern life and the fact that we are being bombarded with information all day, every day. We now receive as much information in one day as our ancestors received in their entire lifetime, and let's face it, most of what you are looking at on social media, for example, is unworthy of your time. All this mind-numbing input is ruining your quality of life and the sense of your own power.

What makes up the content of your mind?

There are some varying figures out there, so depending on who you read, the average person has around 60,000 thoughts per day. According to the Cleveland Clinic, 95% of these are repetitive thoughts (so that's 57,000)—you have them every day and, 80% of these repetitive thoughts (that's 45,600) are negative.

Blimey! Can you see now why a gratitude practice is so important? You have only 3,000 fresh thoughts each day. Why are we thinking the same old negative stuff day in, day out? Because we are not harnessing the power of the thinking mind and have allowed it to take hold of the steering wheel. It's supposed to be a servant of the heart, not its master.

Our minds have gone feral, left to themselves they feast on negative, repetitive junk—binge thinking. Why do we let this happen?

Well, it can really serve a purpose to have your mind distracted and full. You cannot think and feel at the same time. So, our thought addiction can help us avoid uncomfortable feelings—we can numb out in response to feelings that we don't like. Many of us have been led to believe that we shouldn't have feelings and emotions; feelings are a weakness—especially those we label as negative. So, when they do arise, we have been conditioned to control and suppress them. As a result, we use thinking as a distraction, so that we don't have to feel these things which we have been told are problematic. If I am in my emotions, then I am failing because emotions are 'weak' (not my word). It can be overwhelming when strong emotions arise, either from current events or from remembering past events. So, we get busy doing and thinking so we don't have to feel the emotional overwhelm. It gives us the false sense that we are coping, but we're not coping. It catches up with us as disease down the track.

Feelings evolved to keep us alive—our ancient ancestors responded to the impulse to run when the body detected a lion and, in their survival, their entire generational line came into existence, right up to you. (Those who didn't respond to the impulse to run became lion food and didn't get to pass on their genes). Other feelings, such as guilt and forgiveness fostered social connection and emphasised the safety, and advantage, of groups. If an individual didn't respond to these social feelings, they were outcast, didn't reproduce or were dead. In his book *21 Lessons for the 21st Century,* Yuval Noah Harari describes feelings this way:

If the feelings of some ancient ancestor made a mistake, the genes shaping these feelings did not pass on to the next generation. Feelings are thus not the opposite of rationality—they embody evolutionary rationality.

It's time to go against the popular tide and start reclaiming your feelings and start doubting your thoughts.

Each layer is influenced by the content of the previous layer. Your thinking mind is being fed by your limiting beliefs and old wounded parts. When an old belief gets prodded into life, it enlivens all the stories associated with it—the justification, the blame, the history, the catastrophising. This is what becomes those 45,600 negative repetitive thoughts, and most of it is untrue.

Chances are, most days are very similar—you go to work, deal with the same people, the same problems and so on. If your boss triggers you on Monday, chances are they also do it on Tuesday and every workday. If they don't trigger you one day, you are still on guard, expecting it. So, in the routine of every day, these same beliefs are being activated as well as their accompanying stories, over and over again. This is the repetitive nature of your thoughts, fuelled by your faulty beliefs, keeping you from enjoying the actual here and now.

If we allowed ourselves to *feel* our genuine response, rather than mindlessly live from old patterns and their automatic thoughts, we might recognise that we're in the wrong job, that it's time to make a change. That brings up the uncomfortable fear of change, so we stuff the emotion down and stay with the familiar habits of feeling disgruntled at work. We normalise it ('everyone hates work') which aligns with the belief that you don't deserve more. There's no way for the soul energy to flow through and light up your life with all this negativity filling your every waking moment.

Life is not unlike a jukebox. If you press a certain button, you'll get a certain song, until you change either the button you press, or the song attached to that button. Let's dive deeper into what our thinking mind should be helping us to do and how to reclaim it.

Chapter 18
Seeing the Hidden: The Reticular Activating System

The process of change requires you becoming conscious of your unconscious self.
~ Joe Dispenza

The subconscious, automatic part of your mind which is largely unseen for the most part, is responsible for 95% of what you do. Have you ever done something you didn't really want to do, like cheat on a diet, and when someone asks you why you did it, you can't answer because you don't really know? It was driven by a part of your mind which you were oblivious to. Only 5% of what you do is a conscious, logical decision, an intentional action.

If you want to make changes in your life, it's clear that you have to become more aware of what is in that hidden part of your mind. By seeing it, you can decide if it's helping you or sabotaging your intentions. The good news is, you have the perfect filter already in place to allow you to both see into the shadows of yourself and change what you see appearing in your life. By working with it, you can upgrade your decisions and your reality.

This filter is the gateway between the hidden, subconscious mind and the visible world you are conscious of, and it's called the Reticular Activating System (RAS). It's located in the brainstem—the oldest part of your brain and it has three main functions:

1. It activates your fight-and-flight response, that automatic, life-saving activity of the survival system, when what you notice is such a threat that it's time to save your life. Lightning fast, it bypasses the thinking mind altogether because logic is too slow when you need to get into action immediately to escape the wolf.

2. It is responsible for your wakefulness—literally when you are asleep (unconscious) and when you are awake (conscious). This part of the brain will jolt you wide awake when it senses a threat, like an intruder in your home.

However, it doesn't just control whether you are asleep or awake, but also what you are awake *to.* What you notice around you influences how you perceive the world. Do you have rose-tinted spectacles or dark and gloomy spectacles clouding what you see? The colour of your spectacles depends on the quality of your beliefs.

3. Finally, the RAS also governs your focus and concentration—the ability to remain awake to one thing at a time. This is critical for learning new things. Remember when you were learning how to tie your shoelaces? It took so much concentration at the start, now it's an unconscious act.

The reticular activating system is like a gatekeeper for what is brought to your attention and what you can hold your attention on, without distraction. I visualise this part of the brain stem, at the top of the neck as the narrow part of an hourglass.

The mind is a wonderful gift. It gathers all the sensory input coming in from the outside world through your eyes, ears, nose, your sense of taste, and touch. Millions and millions of pieces of information are entering your brain this way every second and this is still just a fraction of the information being passed from your body to your brain.

Your brain lets it all flow in like a giant, receptive, super-computer and only flags up what it thinks is important for you to notice. Have you ever been at a large gathering, or party and it's noisy, you can hardly hear yourself think? And yet, from across the room you hear your name mentioned. How does that happen? All the sound, all the noise is coming into you and being reviewed in your brain. When your brain picks up your name, it recognises this might be important and it alerts you. It is brought to your attention (made conscious) for you to respond to.

Next time you're standing at the checkout in the supermarket, notice how mindlessly the items get scanned, and the constant bleep, bleep, bleep—it's so hypnotic, you can be half asleep on your feet. Then a barcode doesn't scan, you jolt back to life, and it prompts the checkout person to stop, and manually look up the price—they had to do something different. This is exactly how the conscious mind gets alerted—hey, you need to do something with this item.

The RAS is where the subconscious and conscious minds meet. It's the decision-making part of you: it uses body feelings and conscious awareness. In the example of the party, your name was flagged up and you became alert. Unconsciously, you honed your sense of hearing, curious to know what was being said. You may even have been propelled into action, choosing to walk closer to the person so you could hear more clearly. This may have happened unconsciously or intentionally. If they were spreading monstrous lies and gossip, you might have decided to speak up and let them know what you thought of them (or the opposite decision—walk away, hide, and cry all alone in a corner)—all from that one alert. How you respond will depend on the beliefs and memories being activated by what you heard and how it made you feel.

This all just happens, all the time, you don't control it. But we can also programme our conscious mind to flag up what *we want* brought to our attention. The whole outside world in your vicinity is coming into you through the senses. You passively receive it all but what do *you* want to be alerted to, what notifications do you want appearing on the home screen of your mind? What's important to you?

Without *intentionally* programming your filter, your mind will flag up the things which *confirm* the beliefs you already hold in the previous layer (from the programming you received from other people). If your subconscious has a belief that the world is a dangerous place and out to get you, you will automatically filter out all the good and beautiful things in your life because it is only programmed to confirm what you believe is true. You will only see the stories and events that show you how awful the world is—all the violence, the wars, the nastiness, and the crimes. You may be compelled through habit to watch the news ten times a day, every time reconfirming your 'truth'. The good is still there in the world, you just no longer notice it because your filter thinks it isn't important. You literally don't see it—you are unconscious in its presence.

I have already talked about this with the idea of deciding to buy a red mini. In that moment of deciding what you want, you told your conscious mind this was important to you (your new truth), and it set about alerting you every time it picked up that a red mini was in your vicinity.

Change requires you to be willing to feel the truth of the moment in the body: the physical sensations, the emotions, the old, activated memories *just as they are*. This is to become truly conscious of what your body (your embodied wisdom) is expressing in this moment. Is it rehashing old experiences or helping you create a radically different future? If you want that future, it's time to start peering into the shadows and discover what's working against you.

By being honest about your wounds, dents, and fears (we all have them) you shine a light on them. Once you can see something, you can create a little distance from it and reset this filter to now show you something new. Those protective behaviours may have served you well as a child but now you're an adult they are getting in the way of letting the joy of your soul flow out into your life.

An **affirmation** of what you are seeking, in the present tense, programmes the RAS to be on the lookout for it in your external reality, and the acknowledgement of it when you spot it (**confirmation**) helps to embed and integrate it into your sense of self (your self-image or ego). This happens using your conscious mind, but it changes the content of your habit mind.

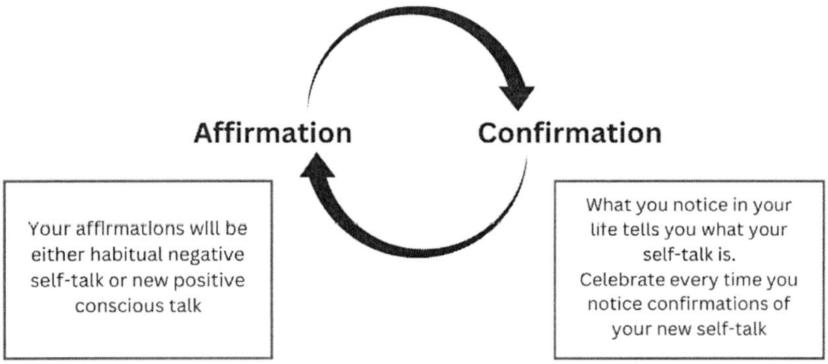

Every time you are willing to be with yourself, just as you are, you are being invited into growth. There is an internal struggle between what your heart wants—to expand into joy, desire, love and creativity, and your out-of-date childhood fears which want to keep you protected—safe, small, and predictable. You can't grow and protect at the same time—so do you want growth or predictability? Now that you're an adult, affirm that it's safe to grow. Explore what safety feels like in your body and it's not uncommon for people, especially those who have experienced trauma, to have no idea what safety feels like. During some phases of your life, predictability might be exactly what you needed…for a while, but not long term.

By avoiding what you see, pretending it's not there, you are effectively saying yes to remaining the same and it momentarily feels like relief because it numbs the pain of the old, wounded part of you which feels unsafe. Changing the protective habits of a lifetime is not a quick endeavour. You cannot simply wave a magic wand and all your vulnerabilities miraculously disappear. There is a process to it though. Start by affirming that it's safe to grow and by welcoming all the separate and rejected parts of yourself. Love them all and put the pieces together. If you want to feel whole again, every part of you gets to be included, not just the parts that are acceptable because they're 'fixed'. Love your wounds, love yourself in the messy process of becoming whole, not just at the end—that mythical place of perfection.

When you become conscious of an old wound, before jumping to suppress it or fix it, enquire into what the emotional need was at the time you were dented and think about a more sustainable way to get that need met, now that you are not a child anymore.

For example, imagine that you avoid deciding about whether to leave your current job and look for a new job, and you find yourself constantly in a loop of moaning about how much you hate your job, you're underpaid and under-appreciated, and you wish you had a new job. It's become so chronic that everyone around you avoids you because you're so negative. You feel so depressed and stuck that you emotionally overeat. You are gaining weight fast and all you want to do is sleep to avoid feeling all this discomfort.

Can you see that the emotional need here might be a need to be appreciated?

Looking back through your life, you recognise this is a familiar feeling and you can track it right back to your childhood when you tried to help, but you were small and still learning how to be a human and you made mistakes. Instead of your attempts at helpfulness being received with gratitude and appreciation, you were spoken to harshly for say, dropping the plates and breaking them, taking too long, not doing it the right way and so on. These things seem trivial to your adult self but being small and being spoken to harshly by someone big, whose love you crave *and* having your desire to help be misinterpreted was very confusing and scary. If this happened a lot, then it created a dent and you learned to protect it with other behaviours, such as avoiding helping others (i.e., avoiding the risk of doing it wrong—don't even try), or excessive people-pleasing (essentially over-compensating by trying to be even more helpful to earn appreciation and acceptance—try even harder) and you probably formed the belief that you were not good enough, there was something wrong with you.

So, now at work, that old wound is being poked—you are feeling all the emotions around not being appreciated at your job. You are right back to the unsafe feelings you had as a child around being misunderstood and once again you feel not good enough. You numb out the pain of all these unpleasant feelings with food which has an opiate effect on the body, making you feel temporarily good, until the comedown which brings with it guilt, shame, and self-criticism later, making you feel even worse. You turn to sleep as the ultimate avoidance of all this dissatisfaction.

You have a choice here to replace the belief and start to look for events and experiences that prove the opposite. Track back through your history and make a list (yes write it down—it will have much more impact, just as in the gratitude practice) of all the times someone said, 'Thank you' or 'I really appreciate your help' or 'You did a good job there, I couldn't have done it without you'. Those experiences are there, it's just that your reticular activating system didn't view them as important because they didn't fit with your story that 'No one ever appreciates me, I am unworthy'. Don't be surprised if you cannot find anything positive—I find this with clients sometimes—they literally become blind (unconscious) to any alternative perspective. In this case, ask others to help prompt your memory.

Once you have gone back through history, continue the practice in the present. Every time someone says, "Thank you," take a moment to notice it. Out loud to yourself repeat the statement "I am appreciated, I am worthy." Do this for a few weeks and you essentially reset your reticular activating system to now start bringing to your attention every time someone expresses their gratitude and appreciation for you.

One way to speed up the process is to say, "I am appreciated, I am worthy" several times daily and throughout the day. Do this every time you pass a mirror (going to the loo is a good trigger and will help you integrate the belief more often).

There's one thing I must make you aware of though. I said before, to change your programming you must bring it up to be seen (which the above exercise is designed to do), and to be felt so that it can be released and replaced. So, this is going to require you to *feel* the very things you have been busy avoiding feeling your entire life. Whilst this can be done alone, I wouldn't necessarily recommend it, especially if you have a history of trauma with a capital T (as opposed to everyday trauma with a small t, that we have all experienced). You want to work with someone trained in meeting these emotions in the body step by step, so as not to risk retraumatising your system again. Slow and steady, focussing on maintaining the feelings of safety is the best way to bring these uncomfortable feelings up, feel them without becoming overwhelmed by them and ultimately letting them go. I also believe body-based practices rather than just talk therapy is best because all trauma is stored in the body and that's where we need the release. Trauma-informed breathwork is my preferred method because you can be in complete control of the intensity of the release, maintain a safe container and let the body do the work without interference from the mind, all guided by a skilled professional.

Chapter 19
Decisions, Decisions, Decisions

A real decision is measured by the fact that you've taken a new action. If there's no action, you haven't truly decided.
~ Tony Robbins

How well do you make decisions?

To have the ability to decide clearly between yes and no; this not that; here not there; now not then; is one of life's learned skills. The clarity of confident decision-making helps us move forward; to live according to our values; and avoid the murky realms of 'maybe' and 'I'm not sure'. Fear is always behind the inability to decide and then move on with life and the fear shows up in your repetitive thoughts at decision time. Thoughts such as:

- What if I make the wrong decision?
- I feel overwhelmed, I don't trust myself to decide
- I can't do that, even though I want to do it
- That feels too big, it could go wrong
- I don't deserve to do/have that
- People might not like me if I do that
- What if I fail?

Many of these will be hidden from view but still alive in you. Of course, you might have all these thoughts doing battle within you.

There are three scenarios which show up:

1. Circular Thinking
2. Micro-managing
3. Perpetual Information-gathering

1. Circular Thinking

In the first camp, many people really struggle and live in a constant fog of indecision, from trying to think their way to a decision, rather than feeling their way using their body sensations, feelings, and intuition. This is a self-created purgatory where you have no clarity to tell your RAS what you want to do because you haven't committed to anything yet. You either don't know what you want at a soul level, or you're scared by it. So, you keep being alerted by the same old things over and over, based on old beliefs, which leads to frustration and feeling stuck. Your soul wants one thing, but you are full of beliefs and ideas about yourself that don't match that. The body feels unsafe with this internal tug-of-war between heart and head, and it freezes—essentially it does nothing, waiting for clarity.

Procrastination is the sister of indecision. Kicking the can down the road you say, 'I'll make a decision tomorrow' or 'I'll do it next week' or 'I'll pursue my dreams when life isn't so busy'. No, you won't because this has become your habit, to push the decision into the future, once again 'protecting' you from the unknown which lies on the other side of committing with either yes or no. Notice if you catch yourself (or others) saying, "Let me think about it," when presented with an opportunity—it might be a social invitation, a chance to be a part of a life-changing opportunity or anything. This is a big giveaway that you are not trusting the body to tell you yes or no. It's a fear response, and a very common one.

Procrastination can also arise from another fear-based behaviour—excessive people-pleasing. Here you put off saying no, or asserting your needs, for fear of letting someone down, upsetting them or from fear of them thinking badly of you and withdrawing their love.

Old fears and associated memories, conscious or unconscious, are uncomfortable to experience again, so you learned very early on to set up protective behaviours around them, so you don't have to feel that mental and emotional pain, ever. The protective behaviour here is *avoidance.* Procrastination is avoiding doing something, and indecisiveness is avoiding making a decision. Until you say yes or no, instead of 'Maybe' or 'I don't know', nothing changes. The result is an inner state of purgatory of your own making.

Without becoming conscious of the old fear and the particular way you protect yourself, your survival mind is set to be on the lookout for anything which threatens your sense of safety. You are stepping onto the bobsleigh run every time an old fear gets prodded and then you get busy avoiding the uncomfortable feelings inside. To live intentionally, rather than through old habits, is to first become aware of what's going on, moment by moment and then deciding to set your filter to alert you to see more of what you do want.

For example, say you set the intention that you want to feel more confident and less stuck in old habits that make you feel unworthy. You can reset your filter to make you aware every time you feel ever so slightly confident. You might use an affirmation like, "I am growing in confidence day by day" as part of your morning routine, repeating it in the shower and on your journey to work.

During the day every time you do something, get a compliment, act in a new way, express bravery—pause and take time to notice it. Take time to recognise this confirmation of your new truth and celebrate it. Give it time to integrate into your sense of self. The more you become conscious of these little confirmations, the more quickly you reset your filter until you don't know why you ever doubted your confidence because it seems to be showing up everywhere…just like the red mini.

2. Micro-managing

Maybe you fall into the category of people who take all the decisions, micro-manage, manipulate other people and events, and need to be in full control all the time. There is no let up and it comes from a lack of *trust*. You essentially don't trust the future, other people, life, the flow, the universe, the unknown or yourself. Instead, you need to make the future as predictable as possible, and you hate surprises!

Whereas the indecisive people have a thought landscape resembling a murky soup of confusion and doubt, the people in this category have nothing but plans, order, and tunnel vision. Both types live in their heads, not feeling anything and disregard the body. They are stuck in their thinking minds almost exclusively, but they are having very different experiences. This group of people (I know this one very well personally) become rigid—in mind and body and tend to be overactive and live at speed…until they crash.

If you're not sure if this is you, look at your body—is it fluid and pliable, or stiff and tense? That will give you a clue. When I acknowledged that ten months with a frozen right shoulder, followed by ten months with a frozen left shoulder was trying to show me something I started to see that it wasn't just my body that was becoming rigid. Two years of being locked down during the pandemic was hard for everyone, and re-emerging afterwards was also hard for many. I masked the uncertainty of reaching out again (I am a natural introvert) and the loneliness of being separated from loved ones (especially my son), by getting busy—a coping strategy I turn to when feelings are overwhelming.

Rather than just allowing myself to be, I used the time and space to cram my head with information. I have always loved learning, but during those two years, I went into overdrive. I trained to be an Autoimmune Paleo Coach because it had helped me eradicate all my Hashimoto's and IBS symptoms and I wanted to help others do the same. Then I trained as an Integrative Nutrition Health Coach, but instead of taking twelve months to do it, I decided to 'use the time' and took the seven-month fast-track program. Then I set about building a new online coaching business to deliver all of this to other people. Don't get me wrong—I love helping people, connecting with them, and coaching them back to a greater state of health and well-being—it gives me a huge sense of purpose, but by the time the pandemic drew to a close, I was exhausted and I was now firmly stuck in overdrive as a habit…hello, two frozen shoulders!

My reluctance to go with the flow and take time to be with what life was giving us all at that time—simplicity, space, and slowness—turned me into a work and study addict and a controlling micro-manager. These are two common protective behaviours where we take it upon ourselves to use our minds to control our lives. We don't like being 'out of control' and having to surrender to a bigger game at play like a worldwide pandemic. We fight against life and leave no space for the mystery and the magic of the unknown to find its way into our lives. Cut off from the juice of the soul, life becomes orderly and dry.

The thinking mind is basically saying, "I am the only one I trust to make decisions" and it's not its job. The mind has decided this is the way my life is going to be, no deviations please—the world and everyone in it must get in line with my plan. This is a life of resistance because the small human mind is no match for the universe. It's also a life of loneliness because no one likes being managed by someone else, so people will tend to give you a wide berth.

The practice of loosening the grip and freeing yourself from old fears and stories that set you on this path is the same as for the indecisive person, paying attention to your triggers, your reactions, deciding what you want more of in life and resetting the filter.

3. Perpetual Information-gathering

The final scenario in the decision-making process is particularly relevant for people living almost exclusively in the thinking mind. For some, the paralysing inability to decide is hidden behind the reasoning that there isn't enough information to make a decision yet. It's really a fear of making the wrong decision—a mistake. By avoiding making a decision this way, you get to avoid the potential blame, shame, rejection, or ridicule from others. Have you ever caught yourself saying, "Oh I don't know, let me do some more research first," or "I can't possibly do that because I haven't studied enough, I don't know enough?"

Fear protects us. We protect our vulnerable parts. The fear of making a mistake, making the wrong decision, and being seen to mess up is a huge fear for many people. It's a form of perfectionism, this unwillingness to fly by the seat of your pants, trust your intuition and be spontaneous. Risks are inherently unsafe and so if your general level of emotional safety isn't there, any additional risk to the small amount of safety you have will be a no go for you. But your soul longs for spontaneity!

The need for more information before deciding, or before stepping into an opportunity is crippling. You want to put even more content in your already overloaded thinking mind in the belief that knowing one more thing will make the outcome of your decision certain. It won't. Nothing is certain, nothing is 100% predictable, it might be highly probable but that's as good as it ever gets. You throw a ball in the air and it's tempting to say, under the laws of gravity, the ball is 100% certain to come back down again. But it could get stuck in a tree, swallowed by a passing bird, taken by the wind. Tiny chances for sure, but enough to teach you that nothing is *certain*. Let go of the search for more information, the illusion of certainty—it's not helping you; it's just feeding your thinking mind's addiction to content. After years of relying on the mind to 'figure everything out' and 'think things through' where has it really got you? Is there more joy in your life? Joy is really the best measure of a well-lived life.

The irony is, if you believe you don't know enough then no amount of knowledge can dislodge that belief. Knowledge is infinite. Only a new belief can dislodge an old one, through confirming the new belief by looking for it showing up in your life—it's there, you just aren't programmed to see it yet.

When you understand how you make decisions and what is sabotaging the process repeatedly, you can replace the old programmes with new ones that you choose. Now when something comes to your attention, you can intentionally respond in a new way, instead of reacting from habit—by asking what does my soul want? Then listen to the body for the answer. This way you create and craft your life wide awake and from within.

One of the ways I make decisions is to ask, "Is this for me or not?" Then I listen to my body. If it lights me up, piques my interest and attention, raises my energy with a full body 'yes', gives me a fizzy expanded feeling in my abdomen, and allows more joy and love to move out from within me then, it's for me. A strong 'no' appears in me as a contraction in my abdomen and is easy to spot. Everything else, including vague responses, also means 'no' because I no longer do anything that is just lukewarm.

When I first began using this to make decisions, I found myself saying no to so many things I thought I 'should' be doing, or that I had 'always done'. However, I followed it, even though I didn't know at first what I wanted; but, over a few years, I discarded what I clearly didn't want. It was not an easy, quick, or comfortable process, but I ended up with way more time available to pursue those things that really were for me, and that allowed me to create what I wanted to create, day by day. I soon realised that all those other tasks were keeping me too busy to do what I wanted to do and, they were not as necessary as my fear-driven mind thought they were.

We often think we lack time for change, for pursuing joy and all the good stuff in life, but we don't. What we lack is attention. We fill our time with so much stuff we really don't need to do and today it's made that much worse due to the fear of missing out (FOMO), social media and the internet generally. How easily we end up down a rabbit hole from our newsfeed, only to lift our heads and realise how utterly pointless so much of that content was. Not just pointless but it amplifies our limiting beliefs and behaviours—we compare, we judge, we feel inadequate, we get angry, we lash out, we unfriend people, and then half an hour goes by watching cat videos to calm down. You say you don't have enough hours in your day, but you don't lack time: you lack focus.

Chapter 20
Attention Is Laser Focus

Focus more on your desire than your doubt,
and the dream will take care of itself.
~ Mark Twain

When you get excited by something you want, and you decide to pursue it with all your heart, the thinking mind can come to your aid. Learning how to focus the mind on one thing—the thing you want to create—will free it from all the distractions and the junk thoughts running on a loop all day, every day.

A distracted, unclear mind is like diffused white light. Think of when you turn on the light in your living room, a soft white light spreads everywhere, no part of the room is left out. The room is full of light. Your mind is currently full of thoughts, all distracting you from manifesting what you desire. But light also has the capacity to become laser focussed, like Superman's red laser gaze. Imagine what you could accomplish if you could have that kind of laser focus.

Well, you can learn how to do this, and the thinking mind is designed for learning new things. Learning new things is just like learning to walk. At the start, it takes all your attention, you fail many times, and you get frustrated, but with practice, it becomes effortless—automatic. Building your capacity to focus can be approached in the same way, which I'll cover in the next chapter but first I want to talk about *discipline*. Groan! I know, most people don't like this word because culturally, we usually relate the word discipline to 'being disciplined' or punished by somebody, or doing something you don't really want to do.

When discipline comes from outside, it often does come as punishment or control. When you think about the origins of the word discipline though, it means to be a disciple of, a follower who is in love with the mission they have chosen to follow. To create discipline is to simply make a choice to do something which aligns with your heart's desire, and to continue to do it for a period of time. (Being disciplined *by others*, stems from their perception: you are not acting in alignment with what *they* value, and they use force to coerce you).

From a yogic perspective, the pursuit of inner freedom begins with discipline. So, if you can't or won't embrace discipline as your friend, then inner freedom will never be yours. It begins with deciding what you want, what lights you up and what you want to bring more of into your life. Having decided that, every moment becomes a choice to act in ways which move that desire forward into existence or holds it back.

Choosing to forge a new way, inevitably means you'll meet resistance from within yourself—the old ways assert themselves, saying, "Wait a minute, we don't do that, that's not who we are." Every moment becomes an opportunity to recommit to how you have chosen to live your life. After some time, the old ways dissolve as you create the new habits which align with the new you and it becomes automatic, just like any habit formation. But, without the discipline of recommitment, nothing changes, and you stay in your old programmes.

Of course, the resistance coming up in you isn't the only resistance you'll encounter. The people around who have been invested in you being a certain way, and playing a certain role in their story, will also get ruffled. We live in relationship with others, we are all characters playing by rules in one another's stories, and you going off script can be perceived as a challenge to someone else. They'll want to bring you back in line with their narrative.

For example, if you have a habit of people-pleasing and saying yes to everyone's demands you will have fallen into relationships with people who like to delegate, which is a polite way of saying they want someone else to do everything for them. As you start to pursue the freedom of saying no when you mean no, rather than saying yes and wishing you hadn't, well you can imagine how that's going to be received by another. As the other person pushes back against this change, you can feel a huge pressure to give up and go back to your old ways. The influence of others is a major barrier which stops people from stepping into their driver's seat. Whether or not you persevere will depend on the strength of your desire for change and how strong your discipleship is to live your best life. It will take courage, and it will be messy as you learn to be an unfamiliar version of yourself. Give yourself time to grow into this new you—you fell on your bum 1,000 times or more when you started to walk, you were robotic and unstable at first, but now you walk gracefully and effortlessly...because you *really* wanted to walk!

There is also no need to force others to change because you are—that would be you trying to bend people to what you value, which is manipulative. Just give those around you time, space, and compassion to start to make their own shifts to accommodate this new version of you.

Periodically throughout the day, become aware of your thoughts and actions, and ask yourself—does this take me closer to the future me or keep me right where I am? Is it confirming my new self-talk or the old, programmed stories given to me by others?

I want to wrap up this chapter with one last point. You may have seen or heard the quote *Where attention goes, energy flows* and it's true. We'll explore more of this when we talk about the next layer, which is the energy layer.

Where you place your attention brings more of *that* into your life, by setting the reticular activating system in the brainstem. When you set your course with your attention, you are announcing to the universe what you want and what you value. It's like setting the autopilot on a plane, the plane will keep going in that direction and when it goes off course slightly, the compass readjusts and brings it back on course: short-term adjustments to meet the long-term destination. In contrast, a scattered mind hasn't been told what the soul wants yet and is idly passing time—like a car with the engine running but not put into gear.

I have a wonderful example of how energy flows where attention goes, which popped into my head this morning.

When I was at university, I decided I would join the university parachute club. I had this illogical idea that it might help my fear of falling! My friend Simon was also game, and so we set off to Salisbury Plain for our first weekend of training. There were no fancy square parachutes with brakes, these were old-school, round parachutes. So, we had to learn to land, bend the knees and roll to the side…the parachute roll!

After drilling this into us for the weekend, we returned the following weekend for a quick refresher and then straight up to jump from a plane.

It was the most thrilling thing I have ever done, floating in the air, so quiet, the view amazing. I had this romantic notion of being a resistance fighter being dropped into France in World War II. Then the ground started to get closer, quickly! I found myself acutely aware of an enormous painted, wooden pyramid, about two metres high that marked the boundary of the landing zone. The landing zone was vast and empty…as indeed much of Salisbury Plain is.

I kept looking at this pyramid, trying to steer away from it out of fear that I might land on it, and we hadn't practised landing on man-made, pointed objects, only flat ground! I kept looking at it and steering away but it just got closer and closer.

I ended up landing no more than ten metres away from it—which is really close! It meant that I now had to gather up the heavy parachute in my arms for the long walk back to the building. I was about as far away from the base as I could possibly be.

We were supposed to jump again the next day, but the weather changed, and we couldn't. By the time the next weekend came around, I had lost my bottle…after all, as great as the experience was, I knew exactly what to expect the second time which only amplified my fear. My parachute days were over. Simon agreed.

As I reflect on this more than thirty years later, I see my mistake. I was so busy giving my attention to what I didn't want—the prospect of being skewered on a wooden pyramid—that I didn't put my attention on what I *did* want—the huge open grassy landing area. Instead of putting all my belief and desire into that, I focussed on what I wanted to avoid, gave it all my attention, and ended up drawing it to me.

We do this all the time, don't we? We want more energy but spend our days telling everyone how tired we are. We want financial freedom but fret about our debts. We want to lose weight but obsess about the scales telling us we're not. We get frustrated, lose faith in change being possible and remain exactly where we are.

I often say that if you can walk and worry, then you can make positive changes in your life. The fact that you learned to walk shows you can learn something new and practise it with all your attention until it becomes automatic. As for worry—this is projecting forward in your imagination and picturing the worst, over and over again…and very often drawing it to you. Worry for the *best* possible outcome instead. Use your imagination to picture and then feel yourself already accomplished in the change you seek, over and over again.

Decide what you want, what brings you joy and focus exclusively on that, with full belief that it's on its way. Keep the faith (i.e., hold your attention on it) until it shows up in your life. When you catch your thoughts indulging in the very thing you don't want, stop, recalibrate, and get back on course to where you want to go. Just like the plane on autopilot.

My actions that day over Salisbury Plain might have been to steer me away from the pyramid, but they were fuelled by my fear-driven attention directed *towards* the pyramid. The energy of fear was firmly glued on the pyramid—what I *didn't* want to happen, and my body was no match for the power of that fear: focussed attention is more powerful than action. When we let the fear of what we don't want, rather than the pursuit of what we do want, direct our attention, we often find we end up with exactly what we didn't want.

Chapter 21
Meditation Is the Medicine

You should sit for meditation twenty minutes a day,
unless you're too busy, then you should sit for an hour.
~ Old Zen saying

Don't groan! Yes, meditation is the medicine for the thinking mind, it balances out the busyness and restores its true function. Anyone and everyone can do it, but chances are, you may have picked up a wonky idea about what meditation is.

First of all, there isn't just one form of meditation and there are multiple stages of meditation. It's like learning a new language. If you've had one lesson in Spanish, you wouldn't expect to be able to pick up a Spanish novel and read the book, cover to cover, would you? You first need to learn vocabulary, grammar, tenses, sentence structure and so on. Well, if you think of meditation as the original language of the mind—quiet and peaceful until it's put to use by your soul—then you can approach it the same way as learning Spanish.

Many people believe that meditation is having no thoughts at all. Well, good luck with that! You may get to that level after hundreds and hundreds of hours of dedicated practice if that's what you want, but even within just a short amount of time you can start to experience moments of deep stillness to balance out the incessant chatter that has become the thinking mind's troubled state.

Let's explore a bit more what meditation involves and maybe you might feel encouraged to bring it into your life. The different approaches to meditation, from my perspective, are:

1. Watching your thoughts—becoming more awake to the actual content of your mind—what are those 60,000 thoughts you're having every day?
2. Somatic (feeling) practices—you cannot feel and think at the same time, so focussing on sensing the body therefore automatically quietens the

mind. Somatic practices include breathwork and mindful movements, such as yoga, Tai Chi and Pilates to name just a few.

3. Attention training—learning to focus and hold your attention on an object of your choosing for increasing amounts of time. This might be:

    - A candle flame or a spot on the wall.
    - A mantra – a simple word or phrase repeated over and over.
    - Your breath – my absolute favourite for its many other benefits.

4. Visualising – this is also attention training but learning to focus on a picture of what you want in the future as the antidote for a mind obsessed with worry and the past. Visualising helps you to create new internal emotional states and new feelings which correspond with the new version of you that you want to create.
5. Connecting to the spaces between thoughts. As the spaces grow and expand you have more access to the experience of being uncoupled from the thoughts moving through you and connecting back to your soul, the part of you who is witnessing the thoughts. You eventually feel a deep connection with the creative intelligence of the universe and no longer separate from it.

Most people think meditation is just number 5, but to jump directly there is like picking up War and Peace in Spanish after that one Spanish lesson. You don't have to make it so hard for yourself. If being hard on yourself is a familiar, lifelong pattern then that's a belief to explore. Some journal prompts might be:

- Where did it come from?
- Who gave it to you?
- When did it start?
- How does this belief benefit you?
- Who would you be without this belief?
- What would you like to replace it with?

Watching your thoughts and somatic practices are great if you struggle with a busy mind that you can't switch off. Attention training is good to build your capacity for concentration and focus, as well as detaching from negativity.

Visualisation helps you re-orientate your thinking mind to what you want rather than what you don't want, and the final path is a place in which to find deep rest and rejuvenation, which eventually arises spontaneously from the other practices. There is no rush to get anywhere. Remember the theme of the book is to unhook from the addiction to speed and end destinations. Think about what you most want from a meditation practice. If you're not sure, if this is all new to you, simply start at the beginning, with number 1, or work with an experienced teacher as your guide.

I have taught various forms of meditation for over the past two decades and the more I do it, the more I have concluded, which shouldn't surprise you, that we make it too complicated! All this complexity, all these different types and ways to do it just leaves people feeling more confused and locked in the belief that it's not for them.

Too many people have said to me, "Oh, I can't meditate. I can't stop my mind from thinking." That's the same as saying I can't eat because I am too hungry. Meditation is the medicine your busy mind needs, and like most medicine, it's not always pleasant, especially at first. Not many people like sitting in stillness with themselves, especially if they feel they can't do it, or they don't like what they find inside. But there is nowhere to get to. There's no degree and no gold medal in meditation. It is simply to arrive fully in this moment, right where you are, as you are and with everything just as it is, free from reactivity. It might be noisy, messy, resistant, frustrating, boring, or exquisite—it's all welcome, it's all okay…just as it is.

Many of us keep our lives and our minds busy as a coping mechanism. Thinking stops us from experiencing our uncomfortable feelings. At first, meditation can trigger all those repetitive thoughts, activate old beliefs that we are not enough, and we are not capable and so on. Ooh, feeling all that sucks so we avoid it by giving up and doing something else to keep us busy…like scrolling social media or scrubbing the kitchen floor. Hence the quote at the start of this chapter. The busier you are, the busier your head is, the more you need the medicine, the right medicine for you. The purpose of life is not to be busy avoiding yourself. The purpose of life is to learn to get back in touch with the true you and learn to love all your parts. To love yourself unconditionally and ferociously just as you are, after all isn't that what you're seeking from everyone else—for them to love and accept you just as you are? But no one will be able to love you to a greater degree than you love yourself.

When I start someone off with a brand-new meditation practice, I first get a sense of where they are, how they are coping their way through life and what they are trying to achieve with meditation. Then I choose a method that will help them the most, and will be the easiest for where they are right now.

Setting Up for Meditation

Whilst traditional, Eastern meditation is done sitting cross-legged on the floor with a straight spine, this is not always an accessible entry point for many Western bodies which have been conditioned for years to sit in a chair. Give yourself permission, right now, to let go of what meditation *looks* like from the outside. Remember we want to live from the inside out, not always referencing what's going on around us and whether we fit in. The aim is to get in touch with what is going on within you. Just because someone is dressed in tie-dye and can sit in the lotus position, doesn't mean they are meditating. They could be thinking about what they'll make for dinner, the shopping they need to do and fuming against their boss who yelled at them today. No one knows the inner landscape of another, so let go of what you think it should look like on the outside and focus on comfort.

A straight spine is a great support for deeper stages of meditation for sure, but at the start you will progress better by being comfortable and relaxed. That might be sitting in a comfortable chair, leaning back, and feeling fully supported by it or it might be to lie down on the bed or the floor.

In my third decade of exploring meditation, I have moved from sitting upright to my new favourite—lying flat on the spare bed. So, perhaps give yourself permission to try that too.

Exercise 1—Getting Familiar with Feelings in the Body

For this first exercise, get yourself into a comfortable position that you can stay in for a few minutes. I recommend lying down or leaning back in your chair. It can be helpful to set a timer so you can let go of worrying about how long you've been there. If lying down causes you to fall asleep, then a comfortable chair will be a better option.

Truly feeling is something so many of us have avoided for years, so don't worry if you struggle with this the first few times. If it doesn't work for you, try one of the later techniques and come back to this another time.

Start at your feet and feel into the points of contact between your feet and the ground. Notice how big the area of connection is, where there is more weight than somewhere else in the feet. Feel left versus right. Give yourself time to explore. This is a practice in mindfulness—of noticing things we otherwise overlook in our busy lives.

Stay in the spirit of curiosity rather than judgement—you can't do this wrong. Simply notice the feeling of connection between the feet and the support beneath them.

Now travel up the back of the legs to the next point you find that touches the support beneath or behind you. Explore that connection point in the same way. Is it a broad area or pin-pointed? Compare left versus right and so on as before.

Keep repeating up the back of the body, stopping to explore each new connection point. Be sure to travel down the arms and discover how your arms and hands meet the support they are resting on.

Finally, feel the back of the head resting. Does the head turn to one side? How large is the area that touches the support? How heavy does it feel?

Then see if you can be aware of all those contact points at once. One technique I like to use is to imagine I am joining up all the dots, like a constellation of stars. Imagine dropping your weight into all the contact points. Allow your body to let go and stay for as long as you like. Your mind will wander and when you notice that, kindly bring your attention back to what you are doing, as if guiding an elderly relative across the road. Simply start feeling those contact points again, one by one, and you'll probably need to kindly guide yourself back many times.

(Notice in this exercise you are bringing curiosity from your deepest layer into the experience. Let go of the thinking mind's obsession with judgement and being perfect. Simply experience the body as it is—there is no need for a running commentary).

Meditation isn't sexy or entertaining, at least not at the start. It can feel boring and dull, especially to a mind that chases novelty and amusement. Feeling bored is not a sign you are doing it wrong—quite the opposite, you are becoming more aware of the feeling of boredom. Stay with it—boredom is a gift we don't give ourselves anymore, we rush to fill it with our phones. Wholeness comes from embracing opposites, so if you tend to have a lot of busyness in your life, explore the boring and lean into it. After all, what's wrong with feeling bored?

Your mind will have wandered from time to time, but all the while that you were able to trace and explore the physical sensations in the body, you weren't thinking of something else because you cannot think and feel at the same time.

If your response to that is, "Well, I was still thinking"—give yourself a pat on the back because you noticed what your mind was doing. It was thinking. You may have been able to hold your attention on the body for a fraction of a second but then your mind went back to its habit—thinking and reporting. This isn't wrong. There is no wrong with meditation, there is only information.

Let's explore what type of things the mind likes to chew on. The next exercise is a technique I learned from a Buddhist teacher many, many years ago and it's still one I find so useful. When we have a thought, we get invested in it and want to carry on a conversation with it in our head. We take both sides of that conversation, and it stimulates so many old stories within us. In this exercise, we are going to take the content of the thoughts away and instead look at the *category* of the thought to stop the inner dialogue in its tracks. It's a great way to interrupt those repetitive inner conversations that just go round and round (and, rather than resisting the mind's tendency and creating tension, this appeals to the mind's tendency to categorise things).

Here are some examples:

- 'I need to pick up potatoes on the way home'—this thought is a **plan** for the future.
- 'I loved my massage yesterday; I wish I could do that every day'—this is a **memory.**
- 'My foot has gone to sleep, am I allowed to move?'—this is a **physical sensation.**
- 'I wish my neighbour's dog would shut the f**k up, I'm trying to meditate!'—this is a **sensory input (sound).**
- 'This is too hard; I can't do it!'—this is a **judgement.**

Can you see how the peace of the present moment gets polluted by the future, the past, physical sensations, emotions, the senses bringing in the outside world and your judgements? Whatever happened to simply being in the flow, witnessing life as it's unfolding and changing, moment by beautiful moment?

Exercise 2—Putting Thoughts in Recycling Boxes

In this exercise, we will start the decluttering process.

Get yourself comfortable, either resting back in your chair or lying down and take a few moments to relax. Set yourself a timer for however long you want to explore. You can start with just a few minutes and extend it to longer as you become more familiar with the technique.

Now imagine you have five recycling boxes in front of you and they are labelled: plans, memories, physical sensations, senses, and judgements.

As you rest, and observe your breathing, begin to notice the thoughts that pop up. Your mind will wander, and you'll forget what you're supposed to be doing. That's a normal part of the process so don't worry.

As you breathe in and out and notice a thought, instead of carrying on the internal conversation, notice what kind of thought it is and imagine you can place it in the appropriate recycling box.

Then go back to observing your breath in and out until another thought pops in (it may happen very quickly!) When you catch one, go through the same process—is it a memory? A physical sensation? Pop it in the correct recycling box because right now you don't need it.

Spend as long as you like here and when the timer goes off, or you decide to bring the practice to a close, remain still for a few rounds of breath and simply notice how you feel.

When you reflect on the experience, notice which recycling box has the most entries. Did you find your mind was occupied mostly with sensory input from outside or physical sensations from inside? Does your mind spend more time in the past (memories) or in the future (plans and to-dos)?

Make a note in your journal and when you try it again tomorrow, make a note again. At the end of the week, notice whether there is a trend or is it random?

Let go of speed and urgency, there is no hurry with this. There is nowhere to get to, other than where you are, right now—fully here and fully aware. Meditation is about becoming present to right now, the only place that life is happening. If you were able to be fully present for ten seconds, celebrate that—build those confirmations that you can do this!

Now it would be remiss of me if I didn't let you know that meditation is what it is. Some days it leaves you serene and at peace; other days it's more like a battle, trying to get a cat into a cat box, when it knows it's going to the vet. I can't stress this enough—this is normal. When you meet the very things you have been busy trying to avoid, expect it to feel uncomfortable sometimes. The urge to stop and walk away may be strong but keep going. Lean into the edge of your comfort zone, don't push, or force or run away, simply notice what the impulse is and make friends with it, sit with it.

Historically, meditation and yoga were taught by men to men. There was also a left-brain emphasis on control. Control the fluctuations of the body, the emotions, the mind, and a lucky few of you who get really good at that, will know peace and joy. Well…that didn't work for me. I tried that for fifteen years and all it did was amplify my already strong habit of trying to control my life to make it safe and predictable.

Controlling our internal landscape is a lot like taking a painkiller for pain. It flattens down the symptoms of pain but when the drug wears off, the pain returns. What if we could discover why the pain is there in the first place, address that, and then there would be no need for a painkiller. Similarly, control without a deep enquiry will only take you so far.

I have come to approach my life the same way. I have gained more personal freedom and more connection to my heart from simply allowing the content of my mind and body to be just as it is, than from all the years of trying to control it all. By allowing, befriending and being curious about it all, it can move through me in its own way. I don't need to react to any of it. I simply hold the space for it all to come and go. It's the *release* of control that is the true gift of meditation. There is more space between what I notice and how I respond to what I notice. I naturally find myself automatically jumping on fewer bobsleigh runs and taking intentional actions, rather than being reactive. I get to drive this vehicle, this life.

Let go, let go, let go of control. This is one of my most common themes when I run breathwork sessions because we are all held hostage by our own control habits. We are so addicted to controlling some aspect of our lives (or the lives of others) that we block the joy and the magic from infusing our days. Use the practice of meditation to get to know your thoughts rather than control your mind. Use meditation to start to hear the dialogue from the body rather than suppress its wisdom. All you need to get better at is *noticing* and then acting in an intentional way in response.

Now that we have started learning how to get better at noticing—the physical sensations and the types of thoughts we have, let's have a go at learning to hold our attention on what we want, rather than giving the mind free rein. Left to its own devices, the thinking mind is like a puppy you let off the lead—it shoots off at a hundred miles an hour, in and out of the bushes, going everywhere and you've got a hard task ahead getting it back on the lead. Sound like your mind on a bad day?

Once again, before we go into the practice, remind yourself that this isn't something you master the first time—prioritise the process over the end result. The thinking mind is for learning rather than controlling. Learning helps you grow and controlling makes you shrink. Learning to hold your attention is going to help you stay focussed on what you want rather than what you don't want and allow the joy layer to flow through you.

Exercise 3—One Minute Focus

For this exercise, you are going to find something to stare at for one minute. Some ideas are a dot you draw on the wall, the corner of a book or table, a candle flame, or the tip of a pencil. Literally, it can be anything. Make it something neutral and convenient that doesn't bring up any feelings. You don't want to choose a photo of someone, or a pen your ex gave you just before you broke up, for example.

Set your timer for *one minute*.

Stare at your chosen object, repeating the name of it either out loud or internally, over and over. When the mind wanders, or thoughts crowd in, simply come back to the task without any self-criticism. Stop when the timer goes off.

For example, if you're using a dot on the wall, you literally repeat slowly 'dot…dot…dot…dot'.

If thoughts rush into the space between the words, then you can repeat them more quickly, leaving less space to get invaded.

How was that? It's not as easy as it seems, is it?

Practice every time you need to empty your mind, several times a day is good, and no one will know you're doing it. Once you find one minute quite easy, set your timer to two minutes, building up to ten minutes if you like. Remember not to rush the process, let go of the addiction to speed and to getting to some perceived end result.

The final invitation is to show you how to use this same technique with your imagination. Imagination is one of the highest functions your mind has and once we become adults, we stop using it effectively. We are under the mistaken belief that imagination is for children. Would you describe yourself as a worrier? If so, then you already use your imagination daily, just not in a productive way. You are using it to imagine the worst-case scenario for the future. You simply need to change the focus of your worry from the worst possible outcome to the *best* possible outcome. The process is the same.

From your enquiries into the ananda layer, think about something that you discovered you want. Let's say you want more energy. Chances are, currently you are filling your thinking mind with repetitive negative thoughts about how your day is going to flow, such as, "I am so tired, how will I get through the day? I can't wait to get home and go back to bed," and this probably cycles in a loop all day long. You are using your imagination to foresee the worst—that you won't get through the day or ever have enough energy.

Imagine that you have a social engagement at the weekend and instead of looking forward to it, you are dreading it because you usually use the weekend to sleep and conserve energy so that you can get through next week. But you know you can't get out of it. Your mind will be filled with thoughts about how bad it's going to be, how tired you'll be next week and thinking of ways you can avoid going. All future thoughts, worrying about what could go wrong.

You can use this same natural gift you have—being able to worry effortlessly to 'worry' about how great the event could be. This is intentional worrying. Try it. Finish this sentence with all the amazing things that *could* happen: What if…?

What if I have the most amazing time?
What if it energises me rather than drains me?
What if I have a great laugh?
What if I meet someone who changes the direction of my life?
What if I relax a bit, sit down, and allow myself to go with the flow?

The old negative stuff will crowd in too because you have a negativity bias, and your reticular activating system has been programmed to confirm your worst fears. You have a lot of familiarity with your old stories, so they are easy to get stuck in. When you catch those repetitive, negative stories crowding in, tell them to 'Go away, we're not going there at the moment' (or use a stronger expression if you prefer…something ending with 'off' is usually a good choice) and go back to worrying about what could go *right*—the best possible outcome. Set a timer for one minute, just like you did with the dot and commit to focussing on what you want to happen.

If you've been paying attention you might think, hang on a minute, aren't we now filling our head with the future, I thought meditation was about arriving in the now? That's true. Whilst you've been focussing on what could go right though, notice how you feel right now. Some journal prompts might be:

- Is there excitement?
- Is there a feeling of possibility?
- Are you feeling creative with your imagination?
- How is the body responding?
- Is there more energy in your system?

Remember that your subconscious mind doesn't understand the past and future, everything is now. Right now, as you use your imagination you are aligning your current feelings to allow more of the ananda to come through into this moment—curiosity, joy, desire and so on. This is the energetic state from which you make your next move, and it will have a different effect than acting from the negative state of dread.

For me, using positive visualisation so long as I also feel it as if it's happening now, is a way to harness my thinking mind's gifts, keep old, unhelpful beliefs at bay and open the doors for the soul to flood through. I try on unfamiliar new beliefs like 'I can make this happen', 'I deserve this', 'I can change the direction of my life', 'I can have what I want'. With repetition, these beliefs will get stronger. Remember it was repetition and emotional impact that saddled you with the beliefs you currently have, so use the same principle for integrating these new ones. Feel the emotion of it being true and repeat, repeat, repeat. You cannot rush this, there is no shortcut.

After you stop visualising what you want as if it's already here, everything has gone the way you want it to—what does it feel like to have accomplished that? You don't have to wait for the feeling of completion—that feeling is available now, as your current energetic reality, and the material world will catch up. Keep doing the visualisation, with faith, until it arrives in your life.

Living from the inside out means you need to know what you want, follow your intuitive prompts, focus on what you want, undistracted, seeing it as completed in your mind's eye as well as feeling it complete in your body. The outer world is on a slower timeline, more resources need to be re-organised and brought together to bring it into form. Keep focussing on what you want in full faith that it's coming, knowing that what you want, wants you.

Part 5
The Energy Field – *Prana Maya Kosha*

Chapter 22
It's All Energy and Energy Moves

Energy can neither be created nor destroyed.
~ First Law of Thermodynamics
Emilie du Chatelet

Everything is energy, and energy moves and changes from one form to another. Energy creates matter. The very things you depend upon for their apparent solidity, like the ground beneath you, your chair, the trees, and so on, are all just energy; condensed energy, slowed right down so that it becomes held, locked for a time into structures and forms.

Think of a mighty oak that has been growing on the planet for hundreds and hundreds of years. So solid and firm, as if it could last forever. Eventually, it falls, we make more solid structures from it, like furniture, fences, boats; but in the end, we burn the logs, releasing the energy held in its tight bonds as light and heat, leaving only ash behind.

Everything in the material world is made up of atoms and science teaches us that an atom is 99.9% empty space. Well not really empty as such—it's vibratory, it's energy. Less than 0.1% of an atom is solid matter—stuff. Yet we focus almost exclusively on this 0.1%, giving it all our attention. The thinking mind sees difference, it separates this from that; my stuff is different from your stuff and is different from the stuff of oak trees. All this difference leads to a feeling of separateness. Whereas the wider, soul perspective (one which meditation can lead us towards) is that we are all parts of one continuous field of energy. That field of energy sometimes takes this form, then changes, gets recycled into another form, and this constant process of change continues for eternity.

All structures, even the most permanent-seeming structures such as the planet we inhabit, are locked in energy and all structures eventually release that energy to be recycled and reused.

You, your body, and your mind are no different. You have so much potential locked inside of you if you could just stop focussing exclusively on the stuff.

I love the 4th layer—the energy layer because this is the layer of transmutation, turning one energy form into another: thoughts into feelings; feelings into sensations; sensations into action and so on. It's where the magic happens and, in my experience, it's the place where the most dramatic changes can occur which affects all the other layers.

In Eastern traditions, the energy of the body was well understood and even mapped out. These ancient wisdom traditions knew, from embodied experience, how energy created reality and recognised it as the vital link between what was inside, unseen and what was outside and visible. The ancient Chinese systems called it chi and the ancient Indian systems called it prana or shakti. Both mean 'life force' or 'life energy' and it's intimately connected with ananda coming out into the world.

Interestingly, whilst these traditions are ancient, they are still in practice today and even experiencing a resurgence, especially in the West, where they are still relatively novel. So often the sophisticated and overly complex, scientific health approaches of the West ignore (even dismiss as irrelevant) the deeper issues at play. They soothe only the external symptoms, leaving the energetic root causes to simply shift and find a new avenue of expression. How common is it to take a pill and get relief from one chronic illness, for another illness to spring up in its place? Before long you are taking a cocktail of medications trying to keep all the symptoms at bay, when, addressing the one energetic cause could clear them all.

Western approaches wait until something goes wrong and then fixes the bodily symptoms, but what if we could prevent things from going wrong in the first place? What if, rather than rushing to fix and control everything after the fact, we could feel the different energy flows in the body and intuitively understand our deeper needs, which are seeking expression and validation?

Let's consider how energy affects form with a visual example: think about those tall slender poplar trees that often grow along the boundaries of fields and roads. If there is a strong prevailing wind from the West, it will cause the trees to bend to the East. Over time, they will strengthen themselves asymmetrically to not get blown over, so they still bend to the East even when the wind stops blowing. You cannot see the wind; you only see its effects. If you had never experienced the feel of the wind against your own skin, you might not even know it exists and your belief might be that all poplar trees grow to one side because that's just what they do.

The energy of the air can cause the shape of the more physically dense structures of the world to be affected and they adapt accordingly. You are part of that world, so energy flows shape you too. The energy layer flows into your body bringing with it either the joy of your soul or the faulty habits and beliefs of your mind. By working with the body and the energy layer, you can get more insight into your own patterns of thought and belief and bring yourself closer towards your true soul. In doing so, you clear the clutter and allow the soul space to shine out.

Practices that focus on the energy of the body are like cleaning a window so the light can come through unobstructed; we might even call it energy hygiene. You don't just clean your window once because it gets dirty again, picking up daily residue and grime. Cleaning the window is a regular practice and the frequency you choose to do it depends on how important it is to have the light shining through. It's the same with you—how much do you want to create, feel, experience, and share love and joy? You decide how often to practice energy hygiene accordingly: if it's important to you, you'll do it daily.

You can see a person's energy and emotions in their physical structures, noticeably their posture. People who are depressed and have low energy slump forward and down, in a physical expression of collapse, as if their body is just too heavy to hold upright under the burden of life. Over time, they may find it almost impossible to stand up straight because their physical structures have been reinforced, hardened to support them to shoulder the burden of life—not unlike the poplar tree.

People who are excited and happy lift their chest upwards, they are animated and light on their feet. People who are wired and anxious are always in a state of movement and can never stand still. In her TED talk, Amy Cuddy refers to experiments which showed that changing your posture changes the neurotransmitter and hormone levels the body produces and affects your mood. Want to feel more confident at your job interview? Go and stand in the bathroom for two minutes beforehand with arms outstretched and legs wide like a five-pointed star. It will increase the hormones which govern confidence and your ability to trust in your own abilities. All our layers aren't just interconnected, they are one living system.

The energy layer is the place where inner meets outer, where the hidden meets the visible. The most subtle, least visible parts of your energy reside in the deeply held beliefs. Beliefs shape your thoughts; thoughts shape your feelings and emotions. Your feelings shape your body and determine the actions your body takes, and your actions create your life.

Beliefs and thoughts are subtle movements of energy—you cannot capture a thought and keep it in a bottle. We can become more aware of our thoughts but as for beliefs, they seem wispy and ethereal, hard to see at all, let alone capture. Once they move outwards to become our feeling responses and emotions, they take on a somewhat denser quality. Whilst we still can't capture an emotion in a bottle they do live in specific parts of the body as sensations. You can learn to recognise the distinct signatures experienced in the body by the full spectrum of emotions from rage to peace and everything in between.

Nervousness feels like butterflies in the tummy. Fear can feel like your bowels have turned to liquid. Your heart races when you feel anxiety and it expands and feels ready to burst when you feel love. You can't have an emotion without a body to experience it. In this way, the energy of feelings and emotions is more tangible and less obscure than thoughts, more real somehow.

Say you were programmed in your early life that the world is a threatening place—perhaps there was a lot of volatile emotion and anger expressed at home, or a lot of criticism and punishment sent your way. Even before you had language, you picked up energy like a sensitive antenna. You could feel the threat to your system energetically and as a way of protecting yourself perhaps you got angry back—you fought and shouted and then ran away. All of this is a natural and healthy response to a threat—it's your fight-and-flight response, designed to mobilise a huge amount of energy for you to defend yourself and live to see another day.

If you got into trouble for fighting back and shouting, you may have learned to internalise the feeling and keep the anger in to avoid more conflict and harsher punishment. With no way of expelling the surge of energy it got trapped in the body, rather than flowing through the body and being released.

The normal, free expression of anger and its surge of energy is for the heart to pound—moving blood to the limbs ready to fight or run. This generates heat. We might become red in the face, especially if we try to hold the anger in. It also changes the structure of the inner ears, so you are no longer attuned to human voice but to predator sounds instead. This is why you can't reason with someone who is angry—they literally can't hear you. It also shuts off the connection to speech. Have you ever been so angry (or so scared) that you can't speak? That's a normal response.

Also, non-essential functions get shut down, such as reproduction, the immune system and digestion—none of which are needed during a fight for your life. Getting to know these physical changes can teach you so much about how you are really feeling in a situation, even when the mind is overriding it with 'I'm fine'.

Children just allow the rising up and expression of their anger, followed by the calming back to neutral once they feel safe again, without attaching any stories or judgements to it. How many times have you witnessed a child flare up in rage and frustration one minute and then play and laugh the next minute as if nothing had happened?

This is what should happen with emotions. Emotion means to e-mote or 'move out'. Emotions are the way the human being expresses what they are feeling inside, brings it through them and out of them, together with whatever energy is required in that moment. It's the way we genuinely respond to life and it's dependent on what is happening around us and how those events activate the deep beliefs within us. If we need to fight for our lives, we need a surge of energy for the physical aspect as well as the courage of a lion to overcome fear. Anger can feel very powerful.

When we want to connect with our loved ones, the expansive outward-flowing energy of love, connection, and resonance with the other person, arise naturally. When we lose a loved one, grief is the same expression of love but turned more inward, since there is no one there to receive and share in it, there isn't the amplification that arises from two hearts on the same frequency.

(As an aside, because anger feels powerful, many people automatically transmute sadness or vulnerability into anger as a protective habit. Sadness can feel passive, downward, drowning and fragile, impotent even. By turning it to anger, it can feel more empowering.)

Oh, to be free in the expression of our emotions! Sadly, the freedom to allow them to come and go is blocked by the content of the previous layers. In the example above, if you hold the belief the world is a dangerous place, you are programmed to protect yourself, but you may also have a conflicting belief that the expression of anger is not allowed in polite society, which leaves you stuck in between. Being stuck can appear as hypervigilance—like a meerkat always on the lookout for threats so you can nip them in the bud and stay safe. There will be plenty of opportunities to self-protect because your reticular activating system will keep showing you things to confirm your belief that the world is dangerous.

Chances are you'll feel angry all of the time, in constant conflict with the belief you adopted from society, that anger should not be expressed. You can't let the energy move through you and discharge it in the designed way, so it gets stuck.

Blocked emotions, from opposing beliefs get stuck in repetitive thoughts. Have you ever found yourself in a loop of justification—a whole novel you can recite from memory, around why it's right for you to feel angry inside? Stuck anger breeds justification, resentment, defence, revenge, belligerence and more…if only it had been allowed to just skilfully flow. Of course, sometimes the anger builds up like a pressure cooker until it overflows and is directed outwards, anything but skilfully, towards another, very often not the person you are actually angry with.

Blocked or repressed emotions which cannot continue their journey through and out of the body will create disease in the physical body and it isn't random. Children who were not allowed to express themselves, take up space and be heard, find they pick up disorders later in life around the throat, shoulders, and neck. Children who often felt insecure and were stopped from expressing anger, often end up with digestive disorders. Children who never learned to 'stand on their own two feet' often develop disorders of the knees, feet, and hips.

It's beyond the scope of this book to provide a full list of physical ailments relating to different emotional states, but if you are interested in exploring this further, I recommend *Your Body Speaks Your Mind* by Deb Shapiro and *You Can Heal Your Life* by Louise Hay.

The default energy to have flowing through your body is the energy of curiosity, joy and love, for this is the energy closest to your soul. Everything else should be a fleeting visitor. That's why I like to start the enquiry from the viewpoint of what brings you joy. What do you desire? What interests you? A life of health, happiness, fulfilment, and purpose is created by living from the soul. But you get stuck looking outward for something to 'complete' you as if you lack the vital ingredients to be happy but lack is not who you are. You have everything you need to live a life of joy and acceptance already, for you are the abundant, creative life force having this unique human experience. It's not about bringing things to you to fill in your dents from the outside. It's about letting the full force of the universe flow out through you, pushing out the dents from the inside. Allow the expansion of curiosity, joy, and love. Looking outward for guidance means you get stuck in the contracting energy of fear and comparison, amplifying your self-limiting beliefs, and handing your power over to others. As you rediscover what you love, and allow yourself to be who you are, you give permission to others to follow and express their joy too. It's infectious. Their expression of joy will be different from yours, and that's okay—it's not about everyone being the same—that's inauthentic and based on control which is a fear-based energy.

Since fear contracts, it creates more density, more structure and more of a sense of permanence—the illusion that this is the way things are and always will be. How attached are you to your beliefs and opinions? The greater your sense of attachment, of being fixed in your thinking and opinions, and that your beliefs are true, the greater the underlying fear. Everything leaves clues for you to follow inward to the deepest source. The energy layer reminds us that *all* things change form. The mind likes certainty and predictability because unchanging forms feel reliable day after day. When life is open to be scripted in any way you like, it can feel uncertain, unsafe and confusing to the mind. So, the mind will attach to anything, such as your opinions and beliefs, cling to them, to help it feel permanent.

Whatever you do to cleanse, clarify, and see the inner workings of your accumulated baggage, will spill over into your body and the life around you. One of my mentors, Samantha Skelly says it's the inner work that's important and it will make the outer work so much easier and more effective. Spend at least as much time on the inner work as your work in the world.

It goes back to how I began this chapter—if you simply suppress a symptom once the disease has appeared in the physical body and in your life, the energy of that disease will just transmute and appear somewhere else and you'll be forever chasing it around. Heal the inner wounds, rather than simply calm them temporarily. Bring the limiting beliefs and destructive thoughts into awareness, see them and get to know them. Release the insidious stranglehold they have on your life. Your body will then start to express new energy, intuition will become sharper, and your life will express that too.

We have already seen the importance of daily practices such as meditation, journalling and connecting with joy, and before I dive into the practice for this layer, I want to emphasise that work on any layer will reveal more clarity around the other layers.

For example, if your body feels tight and you spend some time stretching it, it begins to feel freer and more expansive, which opens the way for the flow of more energy, and more breath. You may not have even realised you had been holding your breath for years. As you become aware of this habit, you may get a flash of insight, an old memory when you felt in danger and held your breath so you wouldn't be detected (this is a normal response in all prey animals—breath holding helps you stay still, silent, and undetectable). Now you are getting glimpses into your survival brain, your subconscious mind, and how you became wired to protect yourself. Breath holding became embedded as a habit which now, as an adult, you do *all* the time, rather than just when needed to survive. It worked once, so I'll do it all the time so I can forever feel safe. No one is meant to live in survival mode all the time. No one can thrive when they are constantly protecting themselves.

Having had a glimpse into your belief layer you decide to stretch your body and unlock your breath every day, and you put the appointment in your diary. Now you have engaged the intentional, thinking mind to help you create a new reality, one where you start to thrive and free yourself from the shackles of the past.

Let's get back to the breath—the most powerful tool at your disposal for transmuting and transforming who you are and how you do life. I taught yoga and yoga breathing for more than twenty years. I always had a fondness for breath practices, even though modern yoga culture has somewhat relegated breathwork to being old-fashioned and boring, focussing mostly on movement practices instead. The yogic practices of breathwork mostly focus on calming the nervous system, ready for meditation and a return to peacefulness and ease. All very helpful.

Modern life means that many people live in a constant state of *nervous system chronic elevation* or *nervous system collapse,* and I use those terms very intentionally. Some words in our vocabulary have lost their meaning and impact. All they do is invite you to switch off and move on. They don't alert your attention anymore because they are overused, not unlike scrolling past repetitive posts on your social media news feed—you stop seeing them and they become background 'noise'. One such word is the word *stress*. We all experience stress, which simply means something that has pulled your nervous system away from neutral and will require a response from your body-mind to come back to neutral again. Your nervous system governs your energy.

Far too many people are living with false beliefs:

1. They believe they don't have stress—only the dead don't have stress.
2. They believe that being in a state of stress and overwhelmed is inevitable in the modern world.

Both limiting beliefs are a form of self-abandonment. You step out of your own agency and slide over into the passenger seat of your life. Beliefs like these will keep you stuck in survival mode and slowly strangle all the joy from your life.

Nervous system elevation is simply your body going up a gear or two. With a healthy, flexible nervous system, this is a *good* thing. When you wake up in the morning, your nervous system is designed to elevate your energy and get you out of bed so you can start providing for your physical needs and the needs of those you care for, such as your children and sick relatives. These needs are for food, shelter, and safety. (In modern life, these needs encompass going to work, paying the mortgage and bills, and preparing food.)

This is you now moving out of neutral (a good stress) and after some time of 'doing', maybe an hour or two, the nervous system naturally starts to reduce your energy back to neutral. It's saying you've done some activity, now it's time to rest and recharge. You feel drawn to take a break, have something to eat and drink, replenish for a while until the energy naturally rises again.

This ebb and flow carries on throughout the day and is linked to the light-dark cycle—your Circadian rhythm. You can trust it to manage your energy throughout the day. With a *healthy*, well-balanced nervous system, within this rhythm, you also tend towards more energy in the morning, calmer energy in the afternoon and deeper rest in the evening and into the night.

Sadly, modern life completely disregards this natural, sunlight-driven flow in favour of the clock. You wake up with an alarm, you must work and focus on your job all day with constant intensity, you don't take more than a quick break for lunch and recharging time is perceived as slacking. Every email or looming deadline ramps up the nervous system without a chance for it to recede back to neutral. All day there is a hidden fear of losing your job and being unable to provide food, shelter, and safety. Returning home, it's now time to do work around the home, still not resting yet. You stay up late, flop in front of the telly numbing out, thinking this is relaxation and then go to bed too late, leaving you in a state of constant sleep deprivation. Tomorrow it all starts again. Sound familiar?

Those few hours with a glass of wine and your favourite TV show are not enough to bring you back to neutral. Deprived of its natural rhythm, day in, day out, your nervous system ramps up and up until it ventures into a zone where it no longer has the flexibility to bring *itself* back to neutral. This is *nervous system chronic elevation.*

This feeling, over time, becomes so familiar that you categorise it as 'normal' because you can't remember anything else; but it's not normal. It's familiar—sure. It's very common—sure. But it's not what you were designed for. Your life is supposed to be about more than working yourself into the ground like a machine, paying bills and barely coping.

There isn't a simple solution unless you are willing to be self-employed and completely in control of your work-rest schedule, which can certainly happen over time; but in the meantime, don't be duped into thinking that there is *nothing* you can do because of your life circumstances. There are steps you can take periodically throughout the day to bring back flexibility and resilience to your nervous system. To not address a constantly escalating nervous system is to lead to the next phase: *nervous system collapse.*

The nervous system cannot keep going at full pelt forever. Once it reaches a level where it can no longer come back to neutral by itself (*nervous system chronic elevation)* no amount of sleep, wine, and telly are going to get you there either. The nervous system is now in a state of dysfunction—habitual elevation; and when it's in this state for too long, it's designed to shut everything down and conserve energy…chronic levels of fatigue occur here, impaired immune and digestive functions, accelerated ageing and more.

This phase of *nervous system collapse* is like applying the handbrake whilst hurtling down the motorway at 70 miles an hour with your foot on the floor. Pause and feel into that for a moment. You come to a screeching halt with wheels spinning, high stress, high tension, but completely static. Now the scenario in your life is more like you can't get up in the morning, you live in a constant fog of poor concentration and no energy, you're jumpy, flipping between anxiety and depression. There is no enthusiasm to socialise or connect with anything because life has become about surviving the day so you can go home and crawl into bed. Socialising and connection need a balanced nervous system and you're not there. Even spending the whole weekend in bed is not enough to get you ready for battle the next time Monday comes around. Whilst you do need more sleep in this state, sleep is not the cure. What you need is to get out of nervous system collapse and restore flexibility to the nervous system. You need to reset the nervous system back to its factory setting.

Having been in that state of fatigue and collapse with undiagnosed Hashimoto's disease for several years, I do not recommend waiting to hit the floor before you start paying attention to your needs. In today's high-paced, over-stimulating, competitive and fear-driven world, nervous system care is just as important to your well-being as nourishing food, movement, and sufficient sleep. It needs to be done daily—just like brushing your teeth and eating. Those things are embedded as habits you don't need to think about. Energy hygiene needs to become an automatic daily event as well.

Let's just pause for a moment and think about where our energy comes from. From a purely biological, academic perspective we might say our energy comes from breaking down the food we eat and using the oxygen that we breathe to make and store energy in every cell of our body. This is true for the 0.1% of you which is solid matter—the structural and biological part of you. The 'food plus oxygen' energy you can think of as a basic, mechanical energy to keep your vehicle (the physical body—the 0.1%) in good shape, like putting petrol in the car. In fact, your car engine works the same way as your cells—it burns fuel (petrol now rather than carbohydrates and fats) in the presence of oxygen to release energy and waste.

But you are not a machine. Unlike your car, you are a multi-dimensional, spiritual being and you also take in energy from other sources. For the other 99.9% of you which is life energy, there are many forms and frequencies of energy that you have access to and use.

The first of these is source energy. The entire universe is all around you and within you. You are not separate from it, however, you can and do set up barriers to it. When you live exclusively in your head, from your fears and all the content you have accumulated in your mind layers, you cut off the flow of energy from the source. Maybe you have no definable spiritual affinity. Maybe you don't feel connected to source energy. Maybe you have never explored it. Maybe it frightens you…what will people think if you suddenly start 'going all new age and hippie or talking about God'—oh, there's a limiting belief right there! Did you see it? What will other people think—such a big block in the belief layer!

You are not a stone, so you will have had momentary experiences of source energy flowing through you. Have you ever had a feeling of excitement, enthusiasm, falling in love, or having a burning wish that came true? Remember such an event for a moment. Notice the sensations in the body. What's happening there? Don't worry if you can't feel it immediately, it can take a bit of practice like learning any new skill, especially if you have been suppressing your emotions for many years.

If 'food plus oxygen' energy is like electricity, then source energy is like nuclear power. Source energy is like having a superpower. When you put up barriers to source energy, you must rely on force energy: hustling, striving, pushing, willpower, motivation, competition all get recruited and it's not sustainable. Forcing constantly elevates your nervous system until it reaches its tipping point, and you collapse, give up, believing success and good things aren't for you. They are for you, but you're going about it the wrong way…as I did for most of my life too.

When you are lit up from *within*, doing something you love, have you noticed that you could do it for hours? You have limitless energy at your disposal. The very next day, doing something you hate, you feel drained and fatigued. You ate the same food, had the same amount of sleep, so why do you feel so energetically different?

Well, in one scenario, you were allowing the joy to flow through you into what you were doing; tapped into source energy which is infinite. In the other, you were stuck in what you 'should do' or 'have to do'. Even the most mundane tasks of the day can be approached in such a way that the joy can still be there—by being the brightest version of yourself in all that you do, even cleaning the floor.

Joy doesn't mean constantly laughing like a hyena and never having challenges in life. It's about acceptance, seeing the value in the task, feeling connected through service to another. You might have the most repetitive and uninspiring job in the world, but when you can truly see it as providing an income, so you can maintain a comfortable home and raise your family whom you love for example, you are invited to engage with your work with that energy. Your job becomes a service, a privilege even. Or you can choose to turn up each day morose and complaining. Which version of you will feel more fulfilled at the end of the day? Which version is more likely to attract new opportunities, get promoted or feel inspired to find new employment they do enjoy?

Your deeper layers: joy, habit mind and thinking mind either enhance or restrict the flow of source energy in your life. Cleaning out the unhelpful content will open the way for source energy to flow through you and there are lots of ways to connect with this infinite resource, some you can do for yourself and some you may need some instruction in:

1. Get outside in the daylight every day. We spend far too much time indoors under artificial light. We take in energy from the sun through our skin and our eyes. Being outside during the day, especially soon after you wake up, also helps to reset your Circadian rhythm which governs all your hormonal releases, as well as your sleep cycle. Everything functions better when you get into the light.
2. Eat whole food not processed food—food from living sources has more life force in it as well as more nutrition.
3. Learn how to ground your energy, especially if you live in your head a lot, live in a big city, or experience a lot of agitation and anxiety. You can do this by being in nature, a park, walking, swimming, slowing down, using natural aromas like essential oils from trees and roots because our sense of smell is directly related to the feelings of steadiness and stability in the body and mind (avoid artificial fragrances since they disrupt hormones and health).
4. Engage in spiritual practices which appeal to you—yoga, meditation, tai chi, chi gong, journalling, sound baths, chanting, singing in a choir, volunteering to name just a few.
5. Be in water more—baths, swimming.
6. Do things which give you permission to slow down. Switch off social media which either keeps you ramped up or numb. Instead, get out tangible things in your downtime which use your hands or your whole body. Try jigsaw puzzles, read real paper books rather than e-book versions on your tablet, dig a flower bed, plant a vegetable garden, make a model, make clothes, knit, cook from scratch, dance, draw, and paint. All the things your grandparents would spend time doing are almost universally good for you too. We free up time by not doing these things but then use that time doing what? More working, more numbing out. There is great mental release in doing things manually and taking your time over them.

7. Use specific breathwork practices to help you connect with the source energy ‘out there’ and bring it ‘in here’. More on this in the next chapter.

Chapter 23
The Breath of Life

A healthy mind has an easy breath.
~ Anonymous

Breathwork is one of my favourite healing modalities for not just the energy layer but *all* layers. For me, it's the one practice that seems to reach everything. It's a practice for life, not a one-time quick fix but it is the fast-track to healing…why?

Your body is a collection of interconnected systems—your digestive system, your hormonal system, your circulatory system, your mechanical movement system and so on. They all work on their particular task, but they also impact and interface with one another: moving your body impacts your circulation which impacts your breathing and so on. Most systems in your body are under the control of the automatic (autonomic) part of your nervous system. You don't have to consciously think about digesting and breaking down your food after a meal, releasing the right hormones at the right time, or repairing the damage to your muscles from your exertions in the gym yesterday—your body just gets on with it.

Thank goodness for that! Imagine if you had to concentrate all your attention on all of that and more, all the time! One slip of focus and oops, forgot to digest that meal, what a waste. Oh no, I have been so busy concentrating on repairing my biceps from the gym, I haven't pooped for two days. It would be so overwhelming there would be absolutely no time for the pursuit of fun.

A lot of your movement also becomes automatic. When you were learning to walk, it required all your focus and attention. Once you have done it enough times, your automatic mind takes over, it becomes embedded as a habit, what we now call 'muscle memory'. Once again, thank goodness! Now you can apply your thinking mind to something new and the learning process begins again. You need to focus on something until it becomes automatic. This is how *all* habits are formed. Taking an inventory of your habits periodically allows you to decide which ones are helpful (they allow for more curiosity, love, and joy to flow through into your life) and which ones need replacing with better habits.

But…

There is *one* system in the body which is *unique*. It is normally controlled automatically *but* you can also decide to consciously take over the reins and control it *voluntarily*—it's the respiratory system…your breath.

"Why is this so exciting?" you might ask. We've all been breathing since we were born after all, and yes, that is true. You have been breathing automatically since you were born to bring in oxygen for your mechanical energy needs, your 0.1% everyday biological needs.

However, breathing belongs to the fourth layer which means it is infused with all the programming and fears of the previous layers. The automatic breathing that you have been doing all your life, is coloured by every limiting belief, doubt, fear, and protective behaviour you have been constrained by your entire life. The distorted breath moves these beliefs and fears into the body as tension, knots, anxiety, depression, and pain.

When you take over the reins and decide for yourself how you are going to breathe, it agitates the whole system and if done skilfully, under the guidance of a qualified, trauma-informed breathwork facilitator, this is a good thing. You can choose to shift your current mood being expressed in your automatic breathing pattern, by choosing to breathe with a different pattern. This new breath pattern will awaken new energy pathways through the body, creating space for new feelings and emotions to be experienced. Changing the breath pattern invites you to experience new ways of being, and brings to light the subconscious memories that have been lurking unseen, perhaps for decades. You can shift emotional and energetic states, explore unfamiliar emotions, and rediscover emotions you have suppressed all your life because it didn't feel safe to feel them. You can bring up and then release old stuck emotions and their associated stories and beliefs.

Our memories, especially those connected with survival and safety get stored in the limbic system—an ancient part of your brain and part of the automatic, habit mind. You are predisposed to store the most emotionally charged memories, many of which you may have experienced before you had words. When the body identifies danger as an emotion, it stores the event in the limbic system.

Every encounter you have, moment to moment, is being compared with this storehouse of past events. When the current event feels similar to a past event (and its strong emotional charge), it raises an immediate self-protective reaction—the same reaction that worked when you were four. It's why it can be so difficult to put into words why we react in the ways we do. Those memories and reactions were developed before you had sufficient words, so there are no words to access now…just a feeling…and your subconscious feelings determine 95% of your actions.

Breathwork doesn't need or use words. It allows those feelings, memories, and old beliefs to be gently stimulated. Just as in the example above, anger needs to move through and out of your body rather than get stuck. All the old stuck energies and emotions can be safely brought up into awareness, felt, moved through you, and released, leaving you feeling cleansed, peaceful and resting in your true soul nature.

Thinking about all the life experiences that you have had, both remembered and long forgotten, it's clear you wouldn't want them all coming up at once. It could potentially re-traumatise the system. That's why it's important to work with someone who is trained in deep awareness and who can help you navigate this process in a safe and titrated way…drop by drop, feeling by feeling. It is totally normal and surprisingly common for people to struggle to start feeling for the first time. If you have spent decades not feeling and relying on thinking to get through life instead, don't be discouraged—you can learn how to reconnect with your feelings and emotions again. Be patient and work with a qualified guide.

Having spent twenty years using breathwork only to calm the nervous system and sensing that there was a missing piece of the puzzle, I was thrilled to find that missing piece. Being able to use the breath to bring things up into the light, in a safe and contained way, means I rarely need the calming yoga breathing practices now. By regularly clearing out all the self-destructive thoughts and patterns, the joy flows more freely even during life's challenging times, and I rarely find myself going into a state of nervous system chronic elevation anymore (and when I do, I trust in my ability to find my way back to neutral).

Using the breath to *just* bring you back to neutral is no different in the long run than taking a pill for a symptom, instead of healing the root cause of a problem. Neutral might feel very appealing to a nervous system stuck in chronic elevation and it is a good place to start, but we're not designed to live in neutral. Neutral is a moment you move through before you get into the next gear, it's a pause. Learning to feel safe moving through all the gears available to you in life is to feel as if you are the master and author of your life. There is nothing to be feared from more energy flowing through you if you're clear on how you want to use and direct that energy. It's only when it seems to come up 'out of nowhere' as anxiety or other strong emotions, that we feel out of control. Being out of control feels unsafe, it's something we don't like. In response, we might have learned to suppress rising energy at all costs. We avoid situations, people, and places that we fear will trigger us and life loses some of its richness as a result. At the extreme, we can experience PTSD (post-traumatic stress disorder) but many of us are living in a moderate to high state of control, avoidance, and fear. Control, avoidance and fear all block curiosity, joy and love and keep you from living your life to its fullest, preventing it from unfolding spontaneously day by day.

So, if you want more curiosity, joy and love and less control, avoidance and fear get involved in your own healing and there is no better place to start than learning all the nuances and applications of your breath.

Quick Check-in Exercise

Sit comfortably with your eyes open or closed, free from distractions. Become aware of your breath and notice how long the inhale is and how long the exhale is. The simple act of watching your breath will cause it to change, you are in that place where automatic breathing and consciously-controlled breathing meet. This is normal.

As it settles into a rhythm, make a note of which part of the breath is longer—the inhale or the exhale. You can make a note of it here:

....

Now check in with how your body is feeling. What physical sensations are you aware of? You might feel pain in a part of the body, there may be tension in your shoulders, is there a feeling in the belly? Make a note here of everything you were aware of (it is okay at this point if you feel nothing at all):

....
....
....
....
....
....

Now close your eyes again and ask yourself what your mood is like. Are you feeling slightly positive or negative? Up or down? Is there an emotion present…maybe frustration or sadness? Make a note of what you became aware of here (again it is okay to feel nothing at all, just notice that lack of sensation):

……………………………………………………………………………………

……………………………………………………………………………………

……………………………………………………………………………………

……………………………………………………………………………………

……………………………………………………………………………………

……………………………………………………………………………………

……………………………………………………………………………………

Whilst everyone's breathing is unique, there are some common associations we observe in the breath, such as:

When the *inhale* is more pronounced our energy and nervous system are more activated, the heart rate rises, and we feel more heat. We are ready for activity and concentration. If this is appropriate because you are busy attending to life, then that's great. But if you are trying to sleep, this would be unhelpful. Increasing the energy further with stronger inhales would be unhelpful if you were also feeling anxious, as this could indicate a nervous system in a state of chronic elevation, where it's unable to come back to neutral by itself.

When the exhale is more pronounced our energy is lower, our nervous system is calmer and more relaxed, the heart rate drops, and we feel cooler. This is appropriate when we are relaxing, digesting, talking with loved ones and ready to fall asleep. It would be unhelpful as you start your day and, early in the morning, may indicate a nervous system that is in a state of collapse.

When both inhale and exhale are equal, it's a sweet spot of equilibrium: there is neither a rising of energy, nor a drawing down. There is just stillness of energy—peacefulness. This is the calming of fluctuations that the yogis sought in their breathwork. In the stillness we are also silent, for the mind also becomes quiet. These meditative moments are the gateways inwards to the ocean of source energy, the 99.9% which is vast spaciousness and possibility, as yet, free from content and unformed. It offers us fresh perspectives as we loosen our identification with the thoughts, beliefs and fears which have colonised our mind and convinced us of their 'truth'. These still points invite us into what more might be available, right in front of our eyes but we haven't been able to see before now, so busy have we been fixed in our own story.

I love these moments! As you drop into the awareness of balance between inhale and exhale, you naturally begin to connect with the points of stillness in the flow of the breath itself; where the inhale pauses to turn and become the exhale and vice versa. There is no need to hold your breath nor try to control it, the pauses naturally expand.

This is such a simple introduction to conscious breathing but it's just the tip of the iceberg. Using breathwork to calm down an agitated system, or enliven a depleted system is just step one. Having perhaps glimpsed a sense of your own infinite potential you can begin to use the breath to unearth, feel and release the content of your accumulated conditioning which, out of fear, wants to hold you back. Your fears were justified in past experiences where you felt unsafe and unseen. A boat is safe in the harbour during a wild storm, but to sit in a harbour forever is not why a boat was built. It was built to sail the seas, explore new lands, and have an adventure! Fill your sails with the breath of life, untie the ropes of the past which bind you to the harbour walls and free yourself to fully experience the voyage of your own life.

Part 6
The Physical Body –
Anna Maya Kosha

Chapter 24
Your Body Is a Marvellous Instrument

Your mind, emotions and body are instruments and the way you align and tune them determines how well you play life.
~ Harbhajan Singh Yogi

Finally, we come to the outer, most dense layer—the anna maya kosha which literally translates as the body of food. Your physical body is constructed from the food on your plate and the liquid in your cup. The physical dimension of you is made up of atoms and as we have seen previously, atoms are less than 0.1% matter. The anna maya kosha is the 0.1%—the physical form; everything else about you is vibration.

Whilst the physical part of you may feel the most real and tangible, in many ways, it's the most insignificant. You are so much more than your physical structure. Your body is where you live, a vehicle you propel. It's not who you are, it's a place animated by your energy, your life force. But its relative insignificance isn't permission to neglect its needs.

Your body is a marvellous tool, an instrument with which you can create beautiful music or a clanging racket depending on how you care for it and for all the layers playing out within it. We can look at the body in many ways and assign it many roles.

On one level, it maintains you in one place. You are indeed infinite creative intelligence, the same life energy that animates the entire universe, but with a body that intelligence, that spirit if you like, can be localised—in you, as you. This allows you to play out your life here and now in your own distinct and unique way. You can concentrate life energy through your personal lens of creativity and find meaning and joy by pursuing what lights you up.

The body creates a boundary between you and all that is not you, helping to establish your sense of identity and agency. Boundaries separate one thing from another, and the integrity of the boundary allows you to flourish, in the same way that a sturdy riverbank allows the water to flow and support life, rather than spill out and create a stagnant swamp.

When boundaries become too rigid, as a way of self-protecting, you create more separation, and it can feel to the soul, as if it's living in a prison. When you become aware of the feeling of being imprisoned, you are invited to look at the necessity (or not) of those walls you've built—the old protective patterns that you're still using today. They worked in the past, but you get to ask if they are still the best way to approach life. Your body should feel pliable and yielding, spontaneous and fluid, rather than rigid. It's not supposed to be a suit of armour.

The body is the interface between you and the outside world, a complex antennae network picking up what's happening in the world around you through your senses and your instincts. Your perception of that world will influence the body's structure and health. As we've seen, the content of your deeper layers shapes your perception: your beliefs, memories, current thoughts, activated stories and wounds, your emotions and feelings are all arising in and shaping your body, every moment of every day to create either greater protection against the world or the softness required to reach out and meet it with curiosity.

When you have a thought, it doesn't stay inside your head. Every thought causes a chemical release in the brain which then travels to and affects all your cells, and you are constructed from those cells. A positive thought full of gratitude and joy will release chemicals like serotonin which signal the body to relax and connect with others. Feelings of anxiety, self-doubt and self-criticism release cortisol, a stress hormone which signals the body to be on guard, ready to defend itself. Cortisol is a survival hormone, not a thrival hormone and you're releasing it constantly from the 45,600 repetitive, negative thoughts that you are having each day.

That's not even the worst part. Cortisol becomes addictive when you are in a state of nervous system chronic elevation, which many of us in the modern world are. It raises the base level—what the body believes it needs in order to function: you end up needing more and more cortisol to get the response required—more energy. Then, when you do start to chill out and relax, cortisol drops below this base level, causing you to unconsciously seek out something to make you feel stressed again so you'll self-release your cortisol drug and get back to feeling 'normal' again—anxious and wired. The reticular activating system is on the lookout constantly to reaffirm that you are stressed, and you need to self-protect (and self-medicate with cortisol).

There are many ways to break the cortisol addiction and the suggested practices in this book are a good place to start. Learning to be with your feelings, without automatically reacting in your rehearsed ways is the key to breaking up with unhelpful habits. It can be as simple as choosing to do something different, such as getting up and taking five deep breaths rather than reaching for your social media feed. As we release the need for constant cortisol hits, the body can soften and feel more at home in that unfamiliar, relaxed state. No longer wearing a rhino hide for protection, the body becomes more fluid and soft. Our attitude to life and the world around us becomes more allowing and more welcoming. As with any addictive habit, it's not easy to break on your own. It's not easy to simply get in touch with your feelings and stop the mind, but with guidance, patience, and a willingness to be free from old cycles, it can most definitely be done.

The first layer, the joy layer, was all about saying 'yes' to life, just as it is. The mind likes to grab the steering wheel and exert control, thanks to the fears, stories, and faulty programmes lodged in the embodied wisdom layer and it's on the lookout (via the reticular activating system) only for those things which confirm its beliefs. Commanded by the mind instead of the soul, the body builds walls of defence, a great big 'no' to life, completely at odds with the soul's desire for joy and to say 'yes'. Saying yes to life just as it is, is to be in a state of receptivity and openness—the vibration needed for growth, curiosity and creativity. It's the essential ingredient to live from the inside out.

Your body also allows you to have fun! It enables you to pursue what you love and what you're good at. It gets to explore the world and try new things—some you'll love and others not so much, but it's how you get to be creative. You have experiences with the body—skydiving, swimming, dancing, standing on your head, sex, sleeping, resting, and it's delightful. You get to explore who you are with a body. You can also use your body to create things which might even outlive your body—art, buildings, monuments, sculpture, books, other human beings for generations stretched out for eternity ahead, each carrying a little of your DNA and a little of your spirit.

Finally, you get to experience all the shades of emotion with a body. From bliss to fury and every colour in between. You get to make sense of yourself and the world around you through the language of your own emotions, the inherited wisdom of all your ancestors. All this happens thanks to your physical body being able to move energy through it. What an amazing gift!

When someone gives you a gift, like a birthday present, how do you receive it? With an effusive 'Thank you!' and a big smile? Perhaps you hug the person—ooh that's another great thing you get to do with your body! Perhaps you vocally criticise the gift—it's not big enough, pretty enough, it's the wrong colour, it's too cheap and so on. If you have ever given a gift and received a response like that, how did it make you feel as the giver?

You talk to yourself like this most of the time. The inner critic is an ungrateful b!*&h and many of your repetitive thoughts might be aimed at your own physical body. Too fat, too thin, too short, too ugly, too clumsy, too bald, too old, too blah blah blah. Your body hears every unspoken word; responds to each shaming sentence with a release of cortisol. It shuts down, protects, feels rejected, unwanted, ashamed and unloved. Is this how you have received this marvellous gift of your body?

For seventeen years, I taught physical yoga classes, and I had a privileged vantage point, looking out over a packed class. Everyone was busy contracting and stretching muscles, trying to fit their body into a shape, such as a downward-facing dog. No matter how skilled they were, how many years of practice they had, every single down-dog in the room was different, unique. In fact, every down-dog you have ever done is unique—your own postures will never be exactly the same, day after day, because you are not the same as you were yesterday. You are unique in every moment and there is no one on the planet, nor has there ever been, who is the same as you. So, who are we all trying so hard to be like? It's impossible.

Perhaps there's currently a celebrity in popular culture who is the latest icon of perfection, but even they don't look like the images on their Instagram feed for most of their day. We get sucked into the ideals we are fed by the media, from peer pressure, and social norms and so we try, try, try to be anyone, other than who we actually are, and add even more clutter to our wisdom layer in the process. All we end up doing is burying our capacity to experience joy even more.

There's an epidemic of self-rejection where the unrealistic pressure to be like everyone else is constantly pressing on our inner wounded parts. We have been brainwashed into saying a huge 'no' to who we are in all our glory, and the result is a growing underlying feeling of dissatisfaction with ourselves and our life: if only I could be like so-and-so, then I would be so happy. It's the wrong way around. Happiness comes from within and it's always here and available right now. It's your job to let the happiness flow *out* of you, not into you from someone or something else.

We beat ourselves up chasing an illusion and we're addicted to it because the body is stuck craving cortisol. We stay in the loop of self-criticism, stress, and joylessness, constantly checking our life and our social media feed for confirmation that we are not good enough. Social media algorithms are just massive external reticular activating systems constantly feeding your beliefs, confirming them so they remain fixed. The algorithms know your patterns better than you do and are keeping you stuck in them. All this external manipulation reduces your capacity to grow, change, and reject the limitations you have been carrying unnecessarily your whole life. When we constantly look outside of ourselves to figure out who we are and where we fit, we're lost. The answer isn't out there. Out there is a place to be curious about, to explore and to play in, but it's not where our sense of empowered self is to be found. A life lived from the outside in, is a life of shrinking, comparing, defending, and disappointment.

You arrived full of your true self, with a marvellous body with which to create beautiful, unique music. It's time to start loving your body just as it is and to give it everything it needs to thrive so that you can feel the joy of living your life to the fullest. The life you see in your mind's eye is yours to pursue but you won't reach it in a vehicle that you're attacking and that's long been neglected. Your cells are replacing themselves all the time albeit at different rates: your gut lining cells are replaced every few days, and bone cells about every ten years. There are parts of your body that are so new they haven't even reached adolescence yet. You can lovingly restore your vehicle, with a little love, attention, curiosity, and patience, so that it can once again become the wonderful gift through which to experience and enjoy your life. Suffering is not an inevitable part of ageing—that's a group myth we have all bought into because that's what we see all around us. A lot of physical disease is largely reversible—you can start to age backwards, by choosing to interrupt the automatic routines of thinking and doing.

I love the phrase: *If you always do what you always did, you'll always get what you always got*. At any point, no matter how many times you have circled the sun, you can choose to do differently—interrupt the unconscious pattern and create intentionally from within, even if everyone else around you has bought into the collective lie. Small new acts create big new changes.

Another one of my favourite quotes is from Gandhi: *Be the change you wish to see in the world.* If you want more love in your world, *be* love. As often as you can, choose to be love, to respond lovingly, to give love to others and to yourself, rather than waiting for it to miraculously appear in your life as you sit in judgement and despair, wailing about the dreadful world we live in. What we see in the world is the result of our collective, historical actions and thoughts. So, to see something new, something different in your life you must become different inside. Feel, think, and act differently to get different results.

So far, this book has explored how the inner layers, the energy of our beliefs, thoughts and emotions flow out into our body and into our life, shaping both. They all play out in the theatre of the body. Since we are 99.9% energy, addressing the quality of the animating flow of the inner world and our connection to source energy is by far the most important work you can do to create the great health and the life you desire. Recruit the 99.9% of untapped potential in order to change the 0.1% that becomes your reality.

By learning to tune into the body with more awareness and more honesty, with a willingness to be with what's there rather than immediately jumping to fix, control, deny, numb, or shut down those feelings, is to honestly receive the information the body gives you. Only then can you see what you really think and feel about yourself and where that originated in your past.

The physical body, constructed from food, isn't just the theatre for the inner world to play out in, it also has some specific needs of its own—its own biological needs—for you to thrive. It's a layer in its own right just like the others, and so it gathers its own content which blocks or amplifies the flow of joy. That content might be aches and pains, inflammation, wear and tear, lack of rest and rejuvenation, chronic illness, presence of toxins, lack of raw materials to build and replace old cells and repair wounds. All this drama leaves the body trying to cope, under-resourced, scrimping on one area to supply another, like postponing wound repair in order to make hormones such as cortisol from the same, scarce raw materials. Under-resourcing the body means that now you can't have it all, even though you were born to have it all. Being constantly under-resourced adds more stress—physical and cellular stress which the body cannot respond to because the cupboards are bare.

It's going to be almost impossible to hear the subtle voice of intuition and wisdom, the soul's longings, and the nuance of emotional energy flowing through you in a body that is noisy with a cacophony of ailments arising from physical neglect—pain, hunger, malnourishment, over-indulgence, lack of sleep, and toxic, artificial chemicals, which your body doesn't know what to do with.

Isn't it time to truly fall in love with yourself and start giving your body what it needs? Because if you don't give your body what it needs, no one else can.

In a nutshell, your physical body requires:

1. You stop speaking to it so unlovingly so that you can release the cortisol addiction—the stress you experience 'out there' in your life is nothing compared with the self-imposed stress caused by your inner critic.
2. Work – your body is designed to move and do things, so give it regular movement.
3. Rest – give it sleep and downtime.
4. Play – engage in joyful, active pursuits that have no purpose other than fun.
5. Nourishment must cover three basic needs:
   - Fuel so you can produce biological energy to run this body.
   - Nutrients so all the functions within the body can run efficiently without having to borrow from some other function.
   - Building blocks to repair the wear and tear in this ever-renewing physical structure.
6. Cleanliness – internal cleanliness means to be free from toxins and poisons.

It's not complex, just six things and yet most of us find them surprisingly hard to do, due to the unhelpful content of the deeper layers.

Chapter 25
You Are What You Eat

You are what you eat.
So don't be fast, cheap, easy, or fake.
~ Unknown

Whilst the quote above may sound a little glib there is a lot of truth in it. Many people think food is to fill a rumbly tummy, satisfy the taste buds and give you fuel. Whilst food does all these things there is another more important purpose for food—it provides nutrients (other than fuel) which is your daily medicine.

Most people these days are eating 'food-like' substances, manufactured in soulless factories and quick to grab as they pursue their complex, high-speed, over-full lives. These food-like substances are highly processed and devoid of any real nutrition—but they're fast, cheap, easy to pick up, and fake. We often eat whilst sitting at our desk, driving, on the run, and scrolling on our phone so that we don't even taste what we're eating…often followed by indigestion. We are not having a culinary experience; we are checked out which is such a shame because eating for me is one of life's greatest pleasures and the easiest way to get my daily hit of joy. Everyone else around us is doing it too, so we convince ourselves it is normal and we are doing the best we can. We're not, we can do better.

We have bought into the collective beliefs (often put out by food marketers) that eating healthily is too time-consuming and too expensive, and my absolute favourite untruth which I was told by a doctor, whom I never went back to is that your food will have no effect on your disease symptoms. It's time to replace these unhelpful beliefs with new ones: it is possible to eat healthily on a budget, it doesn't take all day, feeding yourself well is a priority and food choices have the biggest impact on how you feel, both physically and mentally. If you want to heal the physical body, then adopting affirmations such as these and then looking for confirmations in your life of them being 'true' will help you become free from someone else's story and write your own instead.

Western medicine is a wonderful resource for repairing injury and fighting infection. Its focus is on removing disease once it has appeared, but it's not focussed on creating health and longevity. Fortunately, there is a growing chorus of voices around how to live in vibrant health, rather than merely without symptoms, because the two are not the same thing.

In the vast majority of cases, we become diseased from what we repetitively do—whether that's repetitive self-talk, repetitive unresolved emotions, how we use (or don't use) our body daily and what we feed it—not just the food on our plate, but what we feed all our senses: what we watch on the telly, what we read, who we follow on social media, who we spend the most time with and so on. It's all either nourishment or poison.

In the yoga tradition, vegetarianism is promoted, even demanded in some circles. This comes largely from ancient Indian culture and history and has a lot to do with a culture which was moving away from the historical practices of animal sacrifice in spiritual ceremonies. This change came about several thousands of years ago and has since been blindly adopted as the way to practice yoga—you must be a vegetarian, without any real self-enquiry into whether that actually suits you. Following external dogma blindly is not the path to living from the inside out as your unique self: quite the opposite.

There isn't one perfect way to eat which will work for everybody because we are all different and your needs change throughout your life too. What was a great diet for you as a teenager, may not be ideal now that you are a postmenopausal woman. How you eat in your twenties might be wonderful until you become pregnant and for those nine months, your needs change. How you eat as a builder on a construction site will be different from how you will need to eat when you accept the office management job. This has certainly been my lived experience. I have experimented with every 'diet' over the years—low-fat, junk food, pescatarian, vegan, paleo and autoimmune paleo, and I have finally settled on a way of eating that works for me in my fifties and no doubt it will evolve again at some point. When we adopt eating labels, we trap ourselves in boxes—and there are many to choose from: carnivore, omnivore, pescatarian, vegetarian, vegan, flexitarian, fruitarian, paleo, keto, intermittent faster, fat-free, carb-free, and so on…but you don't need to pick a box, that's the mind seeking to create artificial order over your life. Free yourself from identity labels! (But do read food labels!)

The mind loves a label and a box but what if it turns out that the way you're eating isn't great for you? Once your self-identity has become fused with your eating label it can be very hard to change. All sorts of resistance, emotions, and self-judgements come to the surface such as failure, shame, anger, and more. We get so attached to our food identity, but what if we could become more fluid with it? Wouldn't that lead to more freedom? For many people the answer would be a heartfelt 'Yes' but for others, the very idea of giving up control awakens huge fear: if I am not controlling what I eat will that lead to over-indulgence and a downward spiral?

I find it interesting in myself and in working with others, that when we feel a strong urge to defend ourselves, we know we have a limiting belief at play. It has its hooks in us deeply. Noticing the need to defend our choices is the first step in loosening control. Some journal prompts might be:

- Where does this deep need to defend come from?
- When did it start?
- What is it trying to protect me from?

This is your edge, a place you habitually try to protect but it's also your place of massive growth. Explore it with curiosity rather than digging your heels more deeply into your belief quagmire and you'll be rewarded with insight.

At one extreme, there are people who adopt external dogma around food and create rigid control but at the other extreme, there are people who exercise no discernment over what they eat—their habits are running the show and the addictive nature of the modern diet results in a physical body spiralling towards disease and early ageing. It's very hard to feel the river of joy running through a body that feels like it's falling apart.

Consider how you nourish yourself: do you need more boundaries around food choices or fewer? Both require the same level of self-inquiry as we have been talking about throughout this book. It begins with honestly looking at what is happening, without judgement. Asking yourself, am I intentionally choosing this or am I being driven by habits, addiction and the faulty programs given to me by others? My favourite programme is 'I deserve a treat' whilst disrupting every single bodily process with a super-sized muffin and bucket-sized, sugar-laden drink. Your body does not need super-sized anything.

Back in the 1970s and 80s, we were given the food pyramid as a guide to eating a healthy diet. More than forty years on and we are still being pushed into a low-fat, high-carbohydrate diet despite a library of research showing it doesn't reduce your risk of chronic illness. Having explored my nutritional needs when I was diagnosed with Hashimoto's Thyroiditis, a very common autoimmune disease creating an underactive thyroid gland, I realised that what I was eating, believing it was 'healthy', was making my symptoms worse and leading to new ones.

Now as a health coach, specialising in dietary approaches for autoimmunity, I see all too often the same initial resistance in clients when talking about a 'healthy diet'. The strength of their beliefs which they have carried around food for most of their lives is incredibly strong and no one gives those beliefs up easily. One thing to keep in mind is this: if you are eating a 'healthy diet', then by definition, you should be healthy. If you find you are struggling with symptoms of disease, then perhaps it's time to explore your food choices with fresh eyes and let go of what you have been led to believe is healthy for you.

It is possible, with a dose of curiosity and a lot of patience, to figure out the best way to eat for you and it will be unique—because you are unique. I go through this entire approach, together with recipes so your food remains yummy, in my book *Nutrition-New Story-New You: Cookbook* which I co-authored with Sue Persad-Patel. If you are interested in reducing inflammation, slowing down ageing, balancing your hormones, healing your gut issues, and creating the best nutritional approach just for you, then grab yourself a copy.

The modern diet is highly processed, nutrient-poor and addictive—the perfect recipe to drive up inflammation in your body and develop chronic gut problems. In his book, *Young Forever*, Dr Mark Hyman challenges our belief that decline, frailty and disease are inevitable as we get older. He talks at length about the link between inflammation and ageing and has coined the term 'inflammaging'. Inflammaging is the common cause of almost every chronic illness, whatever your age, so getting it under control is a necessary step if you want radiant health and a youthful body right now and for as long as possible.

Whilst we all have different nutritional needs, there are some basics from which we all benefit:

Hydrate

Adult bodies are 55% water (females) to 60% water (males) and it varies a bit by body type as well: for example, lean bodies have more water content than those with higher fat content. So, we all need to keep this physical body hydrated. Many bodily functions occur in the fluid systems—your blood for example is 95% water and if you become dehydrated then it gets sluggish and slow. Digestion, lymph drainage, and reproduction all happen in fluid systems, so aim to increase your fluid intake by eating more naturally water-rich foods, like fruits and vegetables, soups, and by drinking herbal teas and water. No need to go to excess, as too much water will put strain on the kidneys and flush out minerals, just add a bit more water throughout the day as part of your meals and snacks.

As your hydration goes up, you'll have more energy, better concentration, brighter eyes and skin, better digestion, and fewer aches and pains.

Eat Whole Foods

Whether or not you eat animal foods is a personal choice, with many factors shaping your decision, including taste, religion, culture and so on. Either way, the foods you choose to consume should be 'whole'. That means they have had very little or no processing since they were picked or raised. Whole foods come from nature and are real foods. Nature is abundant and provides all the nutrients we need to thrive, as well as supporting all the other plants and animals on the planet and she does it in a balanced way. Modern industrial farming practices have diminished our soils and as a result, our produce is lacking in many nutrients. But still, a whole food diet is the way to go, perhaps adding a good multi-supplement if you have symptoms of disease (talk with a nutritionist for bespoke advice).

Whole foods are the things you would find available to eat if supermarkets and industrial agriculture didn't exist and you had to forage for your own dinner: animals, birds, fish, eggs, milk straight from a cow or goat, honey, nuts, seeds, beans, vegetables, fruits (some of these would only be available seasonally, especially nuts, seeds, beans, fruits and vegetables). Whole foods haven't been interfered with too much, if at all. Grass-fed steak is a whole food, vegan 'sausages' from vegetable-textured protein, are not. Potatoes are a whole food; takeaway French fries are not.

Let's take olives as an example. The most 'whole' way to eat an olive is picked straight from the tree. Cold-pressed olive oil would be minimally processed, certainly with nothing added and no heat applied which would change the nutrients available. Canned olives, for longer storage, would again be only minimally processed. You don't need to obsess about it but start to notice and look at labels. If there's an ingredient list as long as your arm, much of which you can't pronounce, then put it back and find something with fewer than five ingredients instead.

Compare the example of olives above with two common 'foods' I just Googled:

McDonald's McChicken Nuggets—per the McDonald's website, have thirty ingredients:

White Boneless Chicken, Water, Vegetable Oil (canola Oil, Corn Oil, Soybean Oil, Hydrogenated Soybean Oil), Enriched Flour (bleached Wheat Flour, Niacin, Reduced Iron, Thiamine Mononitrate, Riboflavin, Folic Acid), Bleached Wheat Flour, Yellow Corn Flour, Vegetable Starch (modified Corn, Wheat, Rice, Pea, Corn), Salt, Leavening (baking Soda, Sodium Aluminium Phosphate, Sodium Acid Pyrophosphate, Calcium Lactate, Monocalcium Phosphate), Spices, Yeast Extract, Lemon Juice Solids, Dextrose, Natural Flavors.

Kellogg's Coco Pops—per their website, have thirteen ingredients:

Whole white rice (64%), sugar, cocoa (3%), minerals (calcium carbonate, iron, zinc oxide), salt, natural flavour, barley malt extract, vitamins (niacin, riboflavin, vitamin B6, folate).

Some foods, such as breakfast cereal appear 'healthy' because they are fortified with vitamins and minerals, which are common deficiencies in the high-carbohydrate, grain-dependent Western diet. This doesn't make them healthy—you wouldn't need so many added nutrients if you ate food that is naturally nutrient-rich. Plus, it's interesting that Kellogg's doesn't disclose the percentage of sugar in the product in a transparent way. Some quick maths, knowing that ingredients are listed in order of quantity present, would suggest that Coco Pops are about 30% sugar, setting you up for a sugar crash, the increased likelihood of eating more calories from empty carbs that day, and in the longer term developing insulin resistance, inflammation, weight gain, and diabetes. So, the next tip is:

Reduce Refined Grains and Sugar

Refined grains, such as flours of all types, including wholegrain flours and gluten-free flours rapidly break down into sugar in the digestive system. Sugars get quickly absorbed by the body, raising blood sugar which leads to metabolic disorders and diabetes, as well as weight gain. Excess sugar in the bloodstream then gets stored as belly fat—the most inflammatory kind of fat in the body. Add to that the havoc sugar plays on our gut bacterial colony, its effect on stress and the way it creates inflammation, you have a recipe for chronically poor health and rising stress. Reduce or remove sugar and refined grains in the form of flour and don't be fooled into believing 'whole grain' flours are better, they're not. If you eat whole grains, eat them as 'whole' versions, rather than in their flour form.

Eat More Vegetables

Unless you are dealing with some short-term gut disorders, eat way more vegetables. Most vegetables are rich in nutrients, high in fibre and slow down digestion so you can get the most out of what you eat. The key here is as much variety as possible. You have probably heard the term 'Eat a rainbow' and this is a great rule of thumb—colourful veggies are the powerhouses for health. Some people may need to go slowly when introducing more veggies into their diet as their digestive systems need time to adjust to the changes.

Aim to have half of your plate non-starchy vegetables and one-quarter of your plate starchy veggies such as root vegetables and squashes. The other quarter should be protein. I am a *Nutrivore*, if I need to have a label at all, which means I aim for a nutrient-rich diet. Some nutrients are found everywhere, others are only in animals, and some are only found in plants. So, I choose to eat meat, fish, eggs and loads of vegetables to ensure maximum nutrition without having to rely on supplements for the basics.

Reduce Alcohol and Caffeine

High intake of both alcohol and caffeine disrupts gut and metabolic health, leaving you struggling with energy, poor sleep, and poor digestion. A little of what you fancy is alright unless you notice that your occasional glass of wine is disrupting your sleep and then you may choose to avoid it altogether, but it's a choice you get to make based on what you observe rather than a rule you must follow because someone says so. Coffee and red wine are actually high in antioxidants and can be incorporated into a Nutrivore diet in moderation.

Cook from Scratch as Much as Possible

The best life skill you can learn and teach your children is to be able to cook. Buying food in its least interfered-with form and cooking it from scratch allows you to really know what you're eating. I used to love baking cakes before I went almost entirely grain-free, but I would always get a knot in my tummy (followed by a moment of pretending I didn't notice) as I liberally threw together butter, flour and sugar…there's a lot of sugar in a cake, and once you see it, you can't unsee it. I usually ended up having one slice and giving the rest to others.

This isn't about making food bland and boring, nor is it about overly controlling every morsel that passes your lips. Food choices, whatever they are, so often amplify our deep beliefs and habits. Changing the way we eat brings up in all of us some of these deeper traits. Unless you have an urgent health issue that demands a thorough dietary overhaul, just focus on making one or two changes at a time and use them as an opportunity not only to create life-enhancing, sustainable changes but also to notice the inner talk that arises in response to these changes. It's fascinating.

Food is a touchy subject, it lights the touch paper of self-defence more quickly than almost anything, so remain inquisitive and curious. You might find yourself saying things like "Eating healthily is too expensive." Before you believe your own thoughts, check if they're true. What is the price of fresh liver or tinned sardines compared with a readymade pizza? Both liver and tinned sardines are nutrient-rich superfoods and great for your body, without breaking the bank…whereas packaged pizza…well, not so much.

I like to encourage the people I help to make a note in their journals every time excuses come up about why they can't nourish themselves well. Excuses reveal beliefs, so ask yourself where you got the belief from, and who gave it to you. So often, people think they eat a healthy diet and don't need to make any changes. It's very often a concept rather than reality and I hear this all the time from new clients who just can't understand why they feel so unwell: "I eat healthily," they tell me.

So, I immediately ask them (and I'll ask you this same question now too): tell me everything you ate yesterday. Almost 100% of the time, the response is, "Oh well yesterday was not a normal day, I was busy, so I ended up eating…"

We lie to ourselves to stop us from making changes because the mind fears change. Remember the content of your thoughts is mostly repetitive junk—don't believe everything you hear inside your head.

Assessing where you are is not about assigning blame or making yourself feel bad. It's about seeing what is going on, just as it is, with no stories attached. It's uncomfortable to be that honest, which is why so many people don't have that frank conversation. After all, once you see something, you can't unsee it…and then you need to do something about it. Until a person is ready to do something differently, they'll put up excuses as roadblocks. People often need to reach a crisis point to be ready to change, and sometimes even that isn't motivation enough.

Look at your fears and excuses around eating a little differently: what are the root fears? Some journal prompts might be:

- That you don't deserve to be nourished and treated well?
- That eating differently will be a punishment? Where did this come from? When did it start?
- You'll lose your partner and friends because you're 'odd' or 'difficult?' What is the fear behind this? Where did it come from?
- Why is giving yourself the best resources a punishment? Where did that belief come from? Perhaps you believe you hate cooking or don't like the taste of real food…dig deeper, what's it really about?
- How was food used as a reward and a punishment growing up?
- How abundant or scarce was food in childhood?

There is so much to unpick in this topic and a great way of starting to see some of the unconscious content lurking within you that is running the show, without your permission. You could keep a food journal for a month where you record your thoughts and feelings around food each day.

There's one lady who springs to mind that I had a conversation with about cooking healthy meals for herself. Her immediate reply, without stopping to breathe or think, was "I don't like cooking, I can't cook." As we continued to chat, she told me that she worked away Monday-Friday and spent all of Sunday making up meals to store and freeze for her partner to eat through the week whilst she was gone. Hmm, so she was batch cooking for her loved one, yet telling herself she couldn't possibly do it for herself. She was great in the kitchen! Digging deeper we got to the root feeling which was that she had rock-bottom self-esteem. Deep down she didn't feel worthy of nourishment and attention and until this conversation, she was completely unaware of how this was showing up in her life, week after week.

Good health comes from habits which align with good health: the things you do 80% of the time. There may be some things you do 100% of the time, which is great, but you can still allow for some deviation occasionally too. What doesn't align with good health is occasionally doing something good for your health (the 20%) whilst working against yourself 80% of the time. Small changes, adopted step by step, are the sustainable way to create more life-uplifting habits. Imagine if you adopt one new healthy eating habit this week, adding a new one next week and so on every week for a year. By this time next year, you'll have fifty-two powerful, positive habits that you will have made automatic, through repetition, so that you won't even have to think about them anymore—no willpower needed, no beating yourself up—they just happen. Watch many of your physical symptoms (which prevent you from living a life of joy) simply disappear. I've seen it happen over and over again.

So, the key question becomes: why don't you want to feel great? That's the big obstacle which needs your attention and get to work on that.

Chapter 26
Movement and Stillness

The body will become better at whatever you do, or don't do.
If you don't move, your body will make you better at not moving.
If you move, your body will allow you more movement.
~ Ido Portal

Your body loves and needs both movement and deep stillness, what we might call work, rest, and play. On a purely biological level, many of your bodily functions work best with movement—digestion, blood flow, and lymph drainage to remove waste. A body that doesn't move becomes stagnant, toxic, and stiff. Movement or lack of it creates the body you experience.

If you stand slumped forward, with your chest pulled down, embodying the emotional tone of despondency, the weight of the head gets pulled forward. To make it less of an effort to hold the head up, the body turns the muscles of your upper back, shoulders, and neck into thick, dense straps instead of fluid, mobile flesh. Now it's easier for the body to maintain this physical position and its underlying emotional tone of despondency. The feeling of despondency and burden, which might have originally been fleeting, then habitual, has now become embodied as your reality.

As this person described above starts to move again to free up the tension in the shoulders and release the emotional state, initially they will encounter stiffness. The stiffness may be so familiar that they believe this to be a permanent state and that it will always be this way. It takes time and steady, loving coaxing to release the pattern of physical and emotional holding. If this sounds like you, keep going. As you remind your body that it can move (even a little), that it's safe to move, and it doesn't have to constantly protect itself as if bracing for a blow, it will begin to allow more movement and new emotional experiences other than despondency.

It might not be a joyful process at first. It might bring up feelings of pain, impatience, frustration, worthlessness, old age, resentment, and a need to force.

But as you meet this resistance within your body without reacting to it, with time the body will allow more movement. It will start to feel both delightful, hopeful, and empowering.

I prefer to use the term movement rather than exercise. Exercise can be quite a trigger word for many. It can conjure up images of exhausting yourself in the gym to the point of feeling sick; being yelled at by teachers at school or from well-meaning trainers. It may bring up flashbacks—memories from school of rejection, where no one wanted you on their sports team.

I have always detested running. I wasn't any good at it all through school. I could swim a long distance, I could walk for miles over the hills near our house, and I loved to dance and play tennis. I was a very active child, but I could not run. Most of the school PE lessons were based around team sports and for that, you needed to be able to run. Occasionally, we would have movement to music in the school hall instead, or gymnastics and I thoroughly enjoyed these sessions, but when it came to running, especially outside in the cold and rain, I literally shrivelled up in dread. The PE teacher would choose the two most sporty girls in the class to be the hockey captains and they would alternate picking their teams before everyone (except for me, or so it seemed) would charge off to the pitch, rain and wind seeming to only add to the fun. I was always in the last two to be picked—me and a girl called June.

Now, roll the clock forward about thirty years and I had the idea that running would be good for me, so I decided to follow the *Couch to 5K* program. It started off alright, but when I had reached the part where I had to run for five minutes without stopping, I had a flashback. I was standing, miserable in the rain at the side of the hockey pitch, wishing I could be anywhere else but there. I felt utterly useless, miserable, and unwanted. It came with a full force of emotion which I took into my whole day. I've been called stubborn many times in my life, so of course, I persevered and did finish the running program. However, the day it ended I never ran again because I didn't enjoy a single moment of it. I had done it because I thought I *should* rather than because I *wanted* to. It came from external pressure and my mind rather than my soul, which only wants to do what it loves.

One good thing did come out of it, though. The moment I completed the programme I had a strong intuitive message: Claire, when you put your mind to something you can achieve it. The question now became, what do I *want* to put my mind to—stop choosing things I don't want at a soul level.

Your body benefits from daily movement. The research is overwhelming that even moderate exercise (you don't have to become a triathlete!) reduces your risk of all forms of disease, improves mood, digestion, blood sugar, slows down ageing, reduces the physical damage caused by stress and so much more. And the biggest health benefits occur when you go from zero exercise to a little bit of exercise.

We have innovated and engineered natural movement out of our lives and replaced it with hours of sitting. The more your body sits, the better it gets at sitting…but not at walking, reaching up, twisting and so on. If you're in your fifties like me, or older, think back to your childhood and how much we all moved—not just the children, but the adults too. Did you walk or cycle to school? Getting a lift to school was such a rare event that we squealed with joy when it happened…but mostly we walked, rain or shine. We helped in the kitchen, laying the table, doing the dishes…now it all goes in the dishwasher. If I wanted to talk to my friend, I had to walk twenty minutes to her house, now we flop on the sofa and reach for our phones. Our leisure time was practical—playing games, using our hands, making things, doing puzzles, helping with chores, helping in the garden, washing the car for extra pocket money, walking to the shops when Mum needed extra carrots for dinner. These are just some of the ways we moved naturally throughout the day.

How does that compare with today? How many labour-saving devices do you own that have made you increasingly sedentary? They are all optional. Try experimenting with doing more things by hand and in person whenever you can; your body will thank you and so will your mind. There is a great mental calmness that descends when we are doing something practical and creative.

Creating a ritual around intentional daily movement is also a good idea. I love the power of ritual. When I want to develop a new habit, I always ritualise it. To others, it may look like I am going overboard or being a bit fussy but ritual works. Every time you do the ritual, you are saying, "This is sacred to me, this is important" and energetically, you drop into the moment more deeply and more quickly.

Let me give you a couple of examples of how I used simple rituals to embed new habits. A simple one was that I wanted to be consistent with my natural supplements every day. I have always been a bit rubbish at taking supplements consistently. Initially, I put the pots by the kettle, so every morning when I made tea they were there as a reminder—it worked for a while but then I zoned them out, stopped seeing the visual reminder since the familiar always becomes invisible to us. So that didn't work for long.

Next, I started using a plastic supplement box...but when one of the sections became empty I would 'forget' to fill it back up. Finally, I found a very small dish and every time I was preparing breakfast, I got out the dish and put my supplements and two Brazil nuts into it. I even ritualise where I place the dish on the table—exactly the same spot next to my coffee cup and a plate of fruit. Every day. This ritual has stuck because it has become a beautiful part of my breakfast setup—the table just isn't properly prepared without the little dish, and I always lay the table to eat (another helpful ritual). It takes no extra time; all it takes is attention and intention. I haven't missed a single day since I started using the dish.

Daily exercise is another thing I have ritualised. We might call it scheduling or diarising but essentially, it's a ritual. I do the things that are in my diary, I don't question them. If it's in the diary, it gets done. I have certain days and times when I go to the gym, and others when I go to yoga class, and walking tends to be more of a spontaneous treat that I enjoy on the spur of the moment. I am not super rigid about this, but when I need to make a change—say my yoga class moves to another day—I juggle things around so I can still make it work. Going to these sessions is a ritual. Even the clothes I wear help with the ritual—an outfit for the gym, a different one for yoga. Wearing clothes you enjoy wearing and feel good in all helps.

I had one client who wanted to get exercising again after a serious illness. She discovered that when she went out for a walk, people she knew would stop and chat with her, asking how she was and being very kind and supportive. The trouble was, it was making her walk too stop-and-start and it was taking too long...but she didn't want to hurt the feelings of friends and neighbours who were simply extending kindness. In a moment of inspiration (thank you intuition!), she decided to dress as if she were going for a run, in full workout gear, even though she was walking very gently. It totally worked. People would assume she was 'exercising', and she could send them a cheery wave without having to stop and chat, without offending anyone. That's the power of creating a ritual.

The ritual also adds a level of 'world-class' experience to the mundane tasks of the day because there is a feeling of sacredness around what you are doing, we slow down, we pay more attention, there is a richer connection and mindfulness in every moment.

Bringing more movement into your day is an opportunity for you to bring either: more of the joy layer to life or a sense of punishment and fixing, amplifying the limiting self-beliefs from the shadows of your subconscious.

What movement brings you joy? What do you like to do? What did you like to do as a child? Do more of these things. If you believe you don't like movement, look back at your joy list to see if there are any clues there. Build up the amount of movement slowly too. Have you ever attacked the gym like a bat out of hell for two hours and exhausted yourself? How did you feel about going to the gym the next day? Chances are you weren't raring to go but feeling reluctant at the thought of beating yourself up again. Movement isn't beating yourself up—that's a wound to explore if you have this story around exercise. Movement can be a joy, revelling in the sensations, being curious as you explore new things, being playful rather than strict.

Do more of what you like and in small doses, so you don't trigger that other lie—that you don't have time. If someone is in love with you, no matter how busy they are, they will always find the time for you. Do you love yourself enough to find the time for yourself? [Hint: if you have the time to look at your social media account every day, you have the time to move].

Chapter 27
The Power of Sleep

Your future depends on your dreams, so go to sleep.
~ Mesut Barazany

Do you remember when you were about seven years old, and your parents told you it was bedtime? Did it kick off the ritual of a daily battle? "But it's eaaarrrly! Can't I stay up ten more minutes? Why do I have to go to bed at eight, I'm not tired."

This was my daily dance, like a well-rehearsed tango, perfectly choreographed and always ending in the same dramatic scene—I lost and off I would go to bed, still declaring that I wasn't tired. As soon as my head hit the pillow, I was out like a light and awoke fresh and early the next day to play all over again.

Fast forward forty, or fifty years and suddenly being tucked up in bed at eight o'clock feels like a luxury, a guilty pleasure we might even feel ever so slightly ashamed of. "I love bed!" I say all the time because I really do. I feel so much more alive, alert and in touch with my soul and my joy when I have had a good night's sleep.

Getting your seven to nine hours of recommended sleep is non-negotiable if you want to feel that river of joy running through you. Compared with adults in the 1950s we get on average, two hours less sleep per night. That's huge.

We are, by biological design, diurnal. Meaning we are awake and active during the day and asleep at night. We are anchored into this rhythm by the sun. It's the Circadian rhythm and all your biological processes from your hormonal releases to immune function and physical repair all have their time slot. It underpins your biology and is one of the foundations of health.

Before we had electric lights, we couldn't really see once the sun went down, except for by candle or firelight. Both of these are more to the infrared end of the light spectrum and help to trigger sleep. On the flipside, early morning is a flood of bright light at the blue end of the spectrum and together with rising body temperature, it wakes you up. It literally turns the light on inside of you and raises your energy levels.

Resetting your Circadian rhythm is one of the best, if not the best action you can take to start feeling better in your body and in your life. As dull as it sounds, sticking to the same bedtime and getting up time, adjusted for seasonal changes, is the solution. Get out into daylight soon after waking, within 30 minutes or so and soak in that blue light. Light doesn't just enter you through your eyes, your skin absorbs the frequency and your whole body responds as if plugged into a fast-track charging portal. Keep to more natural light and reduce screen usage in the evenings so that your hormonal system doesn't think you exist in eternal daytime. Once again, the solution isn't complex, but your mind is going to jump in pretty fast with plenty of excuses to stop you from making this simple change: it's what the mind does in response to the threat of change, which it doesn't like.

Today we have the blessing that is electricity and the curse that is 24-hour information flow, from multiple sources, all coming through bright screens and convenient enough to take everywhere we go. Too much blue light in the latter part of the day and not enough red is a recipe for disaster for all those biological systems that rely on light triggers…which is all of them. One example that comes to mind is the glymphatic system—you may not have heard of it as it's quite newly understood. It's a function that happens in your brain. The brain cells shrink, and fluid is flushed through the spaces in between to remove toxins, a bit like throwing a bucket of water over a dirty car. But here's the thing—these toxins build up during the day and can *only* be flushed during deep sleep. By not making sleep as much of a priority as being awake, your brain exists in a kind of toxic soup. Say hello to poor concentration, brain fog, and brain inflammation.

Another example relates to our hunger hormones. When you have a bad night's sleep, it disrupts hunger hormones (and others) and leads to consuming on average, an additional 500 calories the next day. That's just one day. What if you struggle with sleep *every* night? That's 3,500 additional calories per week, which for women is roughly two extra days of food intake, every week. If you know your health would benefit from losing weight, start by prioritising sleep.

Often the real problem with sleep hasn't got so much to do with nighttime but daytime—living in a state of stress, hypervigilant all day, like a rabbit in the headlights. Nervous system chronic elevation makes it very difficult for you to switch off those headlights at bedtime. You remain on alert in the darkness, more so since the darkness is full of perceived demons. You remain ready to do, ready to react, stuck with your foot on the accelerator, ready to run. Don't all worries become giant monster problems when you turn out the light?

Then there is that well-rehearsed tango from childhood. Only now you are playing both sides. Your inner parent might nudge you to look at the clock—it's nine o'clock. Ok, you need to start winding down and get ready for bed. It might remind you that bed by ten or eleven is 'good for you' and try to cajole you into the land of nod. You respond from your well-rehearsed pattern: I don't want to go to bed! I'm not tired, I haven't had a moment to sit down all day, I still have chores to do, I'll sleep when I'm dead, and there's a film on the telly I want to watch…or some other excuse. How steady is your inner parent? Do they cave in and say, "Ok, you can stay up a bit longer?" You are playing both roles here and there are times when your inner parent needs to organise your life, just as there are times when your inner child needs to play.

There's a wealth of guidance online around creating better sleep routines but here are my top favourites, which I use every day:

Keep to Time

Go to bed and get up at the same time each day, even on the weekend, at least within an hour. There will be seasonal shifts since we are tied to the sun. If you live nearer to the equator, there is less change in the length of daylight from summer to winter, but further north it shifts by many hours. You may start to become tuned in to how you naturally start to wake up earlier in the summertime, go with that if you can.

Total Darkness

Light triggers hormonal processes and we are wired to awaken with increasing light. Use dark curtains if you have a lot of light coming in through the window from outside. Scan your room for irritating (and surprisingly bright at midnight) pinpricks of light from electronic equipment and devices. In an ideal world, and especially if you are not finding other solutions that are working, remove all electronic devices from the bedroom. The bedroom should be for sleep and love, so cocoon it from the outside world which will try to inveigle its way in like the creeping tendrils of Japanese Knotweed.

My top tip however is to purchase an eye mask, with a good, folded lip for the nose so that no light can come in. This one small purchase has had more positive effects on my sleep than anything else and an added bonus is you can travel anywhere with it and know you'll be able to create darkness at bedtime.

Keep It Cool

Keep your bed warm by all means, but keep the room cool, which can be as simple as opening a window at night, running a fan, or if you have access to it in very hot weather, running the air conditioner.

Trigger the Relaxation Response

As we let go of our need to be doing, doing, doing as the day comes to a close, the body will naturally trigger its relaxation response in order to set about its night shift duties of restoration and repair, so you are ready for the next day. The body still has plenty to 'do' at night but is free from the overbearing pressure of the mind's agenda.

As you fall asleep your body temperature drops, they go hand in hand. The best way to amplify this is to have a hot bath or shower thirty minutes before bedtime. The body will start to cool afterwards, and you can ride that cooling wave all the way to deep sleep.

Some parts of your diet may be keeping your core body temperature high at night making it harder for you to either fall asleep or stay asleep. The most common culprits are caffeine, alcohol and spicy foods, so consider experimenting with cutting down on these, having them earlier in the day (maybe not the alcohol!) or removing them entirely.

Certain plants produce natural compounds which act upon our nervous system in ways that encourage relaxation and they have been used for thousands of years. Herbs such as chamomile and lavender; trees such as cedarwood and black spruce; and roots such as vetiver and valerian. Herbs make a wonderful bedtime tea. You can add the essential oils of all of these to your bath or your body lotion. Incorporate them into a bedtime ritual that becomes an embedded habit—something you just do without thinking, like brushing your teeth and turning out the light. The scent, together with the activity, tells your brain, "Oh, it's bedtime." The ritual itself becomes the inner parent so you can drop the resistance towards being 'told' what to do.

Medication Inventory

Many prescriptions and over-the-counter medications list insomnia as a side effect. Check the leaflets for all your daily pills and if insomnia is a common side effect speak with your doctor or pharmacist about other options when it comes to prescription drugs. For over-the-counter medications, consider switching to herbal options, implementing some of the ideas here and reviewing your diet for possible causes.

Sleep allows us to play at life, lack of sleep makes us work at life because we are always beginning a new day on catch up: we haven't repaired the damage from yesterday yet. When we're tired, we are more likely to fall back on ingrained habits that we don't have to think about, rather than using creativity and presence of mind to craft our day. Day after day, chronic sleep deprivation means life feels hard, tough, dry, and repetitive. You fall victim to your own inner narratives and nothing changes. It can change, and it's down to you.

To return to the quote at the start of this chapter: there's more than just biology going on here. Attending to sleep is how you keep your car (a.k.a. your body) functioning at its best. But you are also the driver and it's the driver who gets the magic to happen, the driver takes the car on a journey.

Sleep shuts down the thinking and conscious mind and as the incessant chatter in your head becomes quiet, you pass through into the underworld, the dreamscape. There is a layer of consciousness of mysterious quality as you transition into sleep called the *hypnagogic state*. This is where you start to receive information from the subconscious mind. With the thinking mind off duty, the floodgates can open to random images, feelings, physical sensations, like falling or missing your step, all just passing through your awareness. What you focus on and feel as you drop into sleep you take with you into the night, and it becomes part of your wisdom layer. If you go to bed with worries and anger every night, those feelings become programmed into the wisdom layer, making it easier for you to feel worry and anger over and over again in your waking life. It becomes the content of the filter, getting thicker and thicker.

What if, instead, you use your mind to focus on something good, something you want to call forth—bringing your future into the here and now? As you feel it as something already completed, you can anchor into that future physical and emotional state right now, and take that into your dreams. As you drop into the hypnagogic state you're planting the seeds of your future—what seeds are you planting? Triffids or sunflowers? [For any youngsters reading this *The Day of the Triffids* was a 1951 post-apocalyptic novel by John Wyndham where giant Triffid plants took over the world. It was made into a series by the BBC in the 1980s—my formative years].

Don't expect with one good night's sleep, drifting off to the imaginings of your perfect life, that it will show up the next morning. Just as planting a mango seed doesn't give you mangos to eat the next day, it takes time for the universe to reorganise itself to bring the perfect vibrational match into your life. Repeat every night, let go of how it will happen, that's not your concern and is just the thinking mind trying to sabotage your soul. The same power that knows how to grow your entire, miraculous body from a single cell can manifest what you want too, out of the unseen 99.9%.

It's a partnership, a co-creation. You must initiate the process by deciding what you want and stating it clearly. You also make a promise to participate in the process (and you keep your promise) then let go of how it will happen. Listen to your intuition as it brings the steps to you, one by one. Take each step without rushing ahead and let go of impatience and doubt. A mango seed, when planted takes a few weeks to sprout and five years before it bears fruit.

Rather than force and strive to reach what you want for your life, take it to bed. Have a ritual of dropping in, focussing on how it will feel when it's here, let that embed (the clue is in our language) into your embodied wisdom. As you become a vibrational match for what you want, you bring it to you. If you lie awake at night fretting that your life sucks and nothing will ever change…then that's what you are declaring and embedding and ultimately continuing to receive. You get to create by going to bed, and as Xavier Dagba put it, *your dreams are the doorway through which the universe reinvents itself.* Can you commit to prioritising sleep, making a ritual around it, as well as using it to focus on what you want?

Chapter 28
Clean the Toxic Wasteland

The meeting of two personalities is like the meeting of two chemical substances:
if there is any reaction, both are transformed.
~ Carl Jung

When oxygen meets hydrogen, in the right environment, they join and make water. They bring their 99.9% energy with them, and it gets locked into a new form. Everything happening in your physical body occurs through chemical reactions, even movement. There are an estimated 37 billion billion (that's 37 with 21 zeros) chemical reactions going on in your body every second. It's truly astonishing!

The natural chemicals (nutrients) you ingest from your food support healthy reactions and healthy biology. However, in today's chemical-laden world, helpful nutrients are not the only chemicals washing through your body. You encounter an astonishing number of man-made, unnatural chemicals every day and they are participating in the chemical reactions within every cell…but not in a helpful way. Your chemistry is out of kilter with your natural design and your body is becoming more and more polluted.

To return to the quote by Carl Jung, if when two chemical substances meet there is a reaction, then they transform into something new. If those chemicals serve no positive purpose in the body, then their reaction produces the seeds of disease, and we label them toxins.

The body works hard to maintain a healthy balance of chemicals in the body, through those 37 billion billion chemical reactions happening every second, but the body is not designed or equipped to process man-made chemicals which have only been around for a very short time. So, they linger in the body, and we slowly observe more and more low-grade unwellness arising, and eventually full-blown disease. The toxic burden on your body overwhelms its cleaning systems and the 'dirt' backs up.

When you think of toxins, you might think of dirty industrial plants, chemical factories and pesticides, and these are indeed all sources of harmful substances. However, closer to home you are exposed to hundreds, if not thousands of unhelpful chemicals every day from your processed food, cleaning fluids, paints, fabrics, furniture, cosmetics, and toiletries. It's tempting to dismiss these as trivial and assume the danger is exaggerated, but pay attention to what you are using in your home and in your daily routine, especially if you have any kind of hormonal imbalance, inflammation, allergies, chronic illness, or breathing difficulties.

Many of the chemicals in our everyday usage are known carcinogens and hormone disruptors. It's now thought that every person on earth is contaminated, and our bodies may contain up to 200 different synthetic chemicals…all of which are meeting other chemicals and setting off chain reactions of unhelpful change.

Maybe you are doing everything right—eating a nutrient-rich, health-providing diet, getting good quality sleep each night, moving daily, and doing the inner work of unpicking conditioned reactivity and unhelpful habits. But you're still sick. Then spend a year removing as many of the synthetic chemicals from your life as you can. Almost all of them you don't need, despite what the marketing departments would have you believe. If you did need these unpronounceable chemicals, then Mother Nature would have designed them into your structure and your biological processes…but she didn't.

When I got diagnosed with an underactive thyroid gland, I set about cleaning up my home environment. Here are some ideas to start you off:

- Switch from antiperspirant to natural deodorant.
- Switch all man-made fragrances (listed as 'parfum' or 'fragrance' on the list of ingredients) for clean fresh air or essential oils.
- Switch all other toiletries to more natural versions, such as:
    - swap from body wash to natural soap
    - swap from body lotions to coconut oil with your favourite essential oil
    - swap from bubble bath to Epsom salts with essential oils.
- Eventually, I started to make my own toiletries with just a handful of ingredients I could find in my pantry—literally pure enough to eat. It's quick, effective and inexpensive too.

- Switch all cleaning fluids for more natural versions and then have a go at making your own. You can clean just as well without the toxic burden and save money too. You can clean most of your home with lemon, baking soda and vinegar and not much else.
- Check out the environmental working group website *www.ewg.org* to see just how nasty some of the ingredients listed in your favourite toiletries really are.
- Google the Clean Fifteen and the Dirty Dozen lists in your area. They change periodically but the Clean Fifteen list highlights the least sprayed food crops (so these are safe to eat conventionally grown). The Dirty Dozen lists the most highly sprayed crops and it's good to pick these up organically grown if possible.

Having made the switches, new habits were established and now I don't think twice when I notice my skin is a little dry. I go to the kitchen, mix sugar and coconut oil with some of my favourite essential oils and ta-da, a moisturising body scrub for the shower without having to leave the house, wait for a delivery or add to my toxic burden. It may seem like a mammoth task, which is why I suggest taking a year to review what you use, product by product. With time, you are simply creating new purchasing (or DIY) habits which become effortless, like all habits.

It's not just the man-made chemicals that can cause trouble. Your own homegrown chemicals such as cortisol, oestrogen, cholesterol and so on can cause problems if the body can't get rid of them once they have served their purpose; or they are being constantly produced due to fears and anxieties which are not being acknowledged and explored. An anti-inflammatory, nutrient-dense and colourful diet of whole foods will help to support your body's detoxification pathways, together with plenty of hydration, fibre and movement, preventing these chemicals from lingering longer than they should.

The Carl Jung quote at the beginning of this chapter hinted at another source of toxicity—personalities. We encounter people every day and you know, I'm sure, that some encounters leave you feeling positive and nourished, whilst others leave you feeling drained, resentful, bitter, flat, or angry. You don't want those emotions polluting your body too often.

When two people meet, the encounter can be one of three types: neutral, you literally don't feel anything change (there is no reaction); positive, you feel better, lighter, happier, more enthusiastic as a result; or negative. Try to have more encounters which give you a positive feeling. Spend time with people who lift and lighten you up because their presence is expansive and will allow more of your joy to find its way through and into your daily life.

The encounters which give you a negative feeling flood you with toxic stress chemicals. You can do several things with these encounters. It's tempting to avoid them altogether so that you don't have to feel that uncomfortable emotion, but I have found that these people, and people just like them continue to show up in your life. Whilst avoidance can definitely give you the space to explore what's going on inside you, you also need ways to manage these encounters and discharge the harmful effects in the body.

When you get activated by someone or some event, it's a wonderful opportunity—a gift in fact. You get to meet an unhealed part of yourself that doesn't feel safe and needs protecting. You meet an old story and a part of your identity. The ways in which you protect yourself are your deeply ingrained coping habits which were once useful but now keep you stuck in repetitive behaviours every time you meet the same type of trigger. When you notice you have been triggered by someone or something (to use Carl Jung's expression—you have been transformed—you were calm and now you're angry for example) you can choose to pause.

Every shift in your state comes with the creation and cascade of chemicals, flooding the body with what it needs in order to fight, run away, connect, or relax. This is a moment of opportunity, to observe and then choose a different response and begin to break the addiction to old modes of coping. Coping comes from fear and protection, dictated by the past. When triggering occurs, it's time to get curious about what's really going on. Ask yourself where this wound came from and what you are really trying to protect. Then get creative about how you might respond differently, from a stance of love and compassion even. Both curiosity and creativity are aspects of the joy layer, so by making this intentional switch, away from the habitual reaction to external circumstances, you step into the power of living from the inside out.

This level of self-awareness grows the more you do it. It's the same process when you notice discomfort in your gut after eating. What food have you eaten that your body received as poison rather than nourishment? Then observe the conditioned reaction that arises when you consider taking this food out of your diet for a week to see how it affects you. Chances are a wall of resistance arises, excuses, denial and justification appear as your inner narrative to stop you from making those positive changes. Your fear-based, subconscious sense of identity has been threatened and it digs in its heels. But your sense of identity, your ego if you like, is not real, it's a collection of past stories and experiences that it wants to make permanent long into the future. But we live in a world of impermanence—every breath comes and goes, every thought, each day dissolves into night. Nothing is permanent, but the ego is in denial. It's why we want to get back in touch with the soul, through the body and let that direct our lives—from a place of grace and flow, rather than rigidity and protection.

Everything coming to you from the outside world and everything arising within you has one of the three effects already mentioned:

- There is no reaction—it's a neutral encounter.
- There is a positive reaction—this is experienced as expansion, lightness, freedom, ease, comfort, health, well-being, and nourishment. Pursue more of this to live a life of joy and creativity, especially to balance out all the negative encounters you have each day.
- There is a negative reaction—experienced as contraction, defence, tension, pain, rigidity, disease, fatigue, fixed stories, justification, and shadow emotions such as shame and blame.

Be willing to be with the negative, to see it and befriend it even, rather than push it away. This invites you into a deeper conversation about your wounds and how you have been conditioned to protect them. Lean into that so you can start to create new ways of getting your emotional needs met, based on the here and now, rather than the past. This is growth and it's how you can turn a toxin into a nutrient for your soul. Once the wound learns a new way of getting what it needs, the old narratives, the old addictive behaviours and stuck patterns can naturally start to dissolve.

Part 7
Putting It into Practice

Chapter 29
Circling Back

What you want, wants you.
~ Mark Victor Hansen

Congratulations on reaching the end of this book! At the start of the book, I said that I didn't want to fill your head with more information—we already have too much information clogging up our layers. I know at times, there may have been a lot of new ideas to digest, but my sincerest wish is that the ideas in this book are slowly put into practice. After all, knowledge is not power. The power lies in the new actions you take because of the new knowledge.

Circling back to the joy layer, let me ask you again:

- What do you want?
- What do you love to do?
- What comes naturally to you?
- How did you love to spend your time when you were a child?

Those things are in you and want you to pursue them. They are only in you, no one else, so that you and only you, can have the exquisite bliss of making them real in your life. If you don't claim them, then nobody will and they remain just ideas, wishes, and unfulfilled dreams.

If what you are experiencing in life isn't seasoned with feelings of bliss, peace, and fulfilment, then you have accumulated something that isn't you. Have you ever bought an item of clothing on a whim because perhaps you were feeling down, invisible, or simply fed up? It hangs in your wardrobe for months and every time you go to put it on you take it off again, saying "It's not me." When we act from low energy states, from acquired programmes, we create something that isn't a reflection of who we truly are, rather who we think we should be…or worse, who *others* think we should be.

We all accumulate beliefs, ideas, thoughts and habits from other people and their expectations but they're not you. You are the bright, full, silver ball with your own unique desires, loves and natural abilities. You accumulated dents and wounds along the way, and the power of habit is so strong that you will continue to go through life, feeling mildly (or massively) dissatisfied, busy protecting those dents, until you decide that you want to push them back out from the inside and return once again, to fullness. Can you imagine having no old wounds, nothing in need of protection? Simply existing and responding to life, moment to moment? Nobody can do it but you because it's an inside job. Sure, people can help you. We all need loved ones and mentors to guide us, people who will hold up a mirror for us to see into our own shadows and those places within which are so familiar we cease to even see them anymore. Someone else can hold up the mirror but only *you* can look at it and do the inner work.

What would it mean to you and the quality of your life, if you could reclaim yourself, the version of you who arrived here on the day of your birth? What would it mean to bring the joy of spontaneity into every day and pursue the things which truly light you up? Would your life feel better or worse? Notice the stories that crowd in immediately: stories like 'That would feel really selfish' or 'It's too late for me, I'm too old to change' or 'It's too hard, my life isn't so bad really'. These all come from your embodied wisdom, self-identity layer: the personality you have created from the meaning you brought to all your past experiences. You're not living backwards. You're moving forward into the next unknown moment. Everything changes, everything ahead cannot be fully known, only predicted at best. The mind craves certainty, but it doesn't exist. The mind has become identified with just the 0.1% of you and your life that it can see: the accumulation of the past, repeated over and over again.

What if you could set all of that down on the floor and invite yourself to turn your attention to the 99.9% of you that you have been ignoring for your whole life: the unformed creative potential? What if you did something different today? What kind of life would you craft from here onwards? Who would you be?

To decide to follow a life of creativity and agency is to recognise that you are currently sitting in the passenger seat and the driver's seat is empty or occupied by someone else…someone who might not even be alive anymore. Change seats and get into gear. You do not need to know the whole journey—

that's another trick of the over-anxious mind—the part of you that only feels safe in certainty. You cannot grow and create something new when you are driven by protection and outdated repetition.

This book doesn't offer a quick fix or a complicated solution. Instead, I hope to offer you a guide by which to craft your life's work—you.

There is no hurry, in fact, being in a hurry will get in the way. If you are willing to slow down, pay attention to what is going on within you and around you, and open yourself to trying to do things differently, to fail sometimes and pick yourself back up, then you can indeed write your own life story from here on in. Rather than living a life of reactivity—defending yourself from life coming *at you,* you can live from the inside out, driven by what you love, what you value, and what brings you joy, rooted in the wellspring of your own soul.

Living from the inside out is deciding to pursue a foundation of joy and agency, to allow life to unfold in its magnificent way and to listen to the prompts of your intuition as it guides you to take the next step. You begin to emit a higher frequency of energy that attracts other high-frequency people and opportunities to you. Life becomes more spontaneous, more delightful, more serendipitous. There is more ease and flow and more trust that all is happening *for* you rather than *to* you. Instead of living from your excuses you live from a sense of 'Let's give it a try'.

It doesn't mean you'll inhabit a world of rainbows and unicorns, that nothing challenging will ever happen again and you'll always get your own way. Living from the inside out is a reminder that within the challenge you are always free to choose your perspective, and your peace of mind, if not always your actions. When things don't turn out the way your agenda wanted, you can recognise that there is a good reason and perhaps you are being redirected towards something even better.

Living from the inside out means to look at why you are resisting what is happening right now; to stop trying to orchestrate your life down to the finest detail; to stop being afraid of the future, of surprises and instead embody openness and receptivity. You start the day from a place of already having received a gift, the energy of gratitude. There is nothing you need to 'get' as you go into your day. Instead, the day becomes an artful opportunity to repay the gift, to give back generously from that huge reservoir of soul energy that is your true self. Who could benefit from a cup of your energy today? How much more help can you be when you are lit up like a Catherine Wheel, rather than a small smouldering ember, defensively beginning your day, trying to protect what little energy and life you feel you have? How much help are you really being as you run on empty, directed by the accumulated programming other people gave you?

If you resonate with the idea of becoming that bright shiny silver ball again, lit up from within and writing your own next chapter of your life, then I implore you not to put this book down and forget about it. You are your own life's work. You are creating your own story and let this book be your companion—your handbook for happiness.

My suggestion is that you go back to the start of this book and begin again, but this time go slowly. Do all the exercises in the book and take your time over them. Drop me an email and I will send you recordings of all the meditations in this book so you can relax and be guided through them.

Spend a month cultivating a new habit before bringing in a new one. Every day is an opportunity to look at yourself and see the content of your layers, and with time you will naturally start to see how to clean away that content. Let your intuition be your guide. It might prompt you to work with a particular therapist, bodyworker, breath worker, personal trainer, or nutritionist. Follow your intuition, especially when you can't explain why it feels right to follow it (in fact if you can explain it, then it's not your intuition, it's your thinking mind).

Some practices, maybe the gratitude practice, will feel supportive almost immediately; others may raise a wall of resistance. Simply be with that, without rushing to push it away or destroy the resistance. As well as the ideas in this book, you'll likely find your own ways of cleaning the content of your layers on a daily basis, practices that work just for you.

As deep changes occur (in the habit layer particularly), there will be periods of feeling out of sorts, as if you have stirred things up and wish you hadn't. Find someone to be that steady mirror for you during these times. It is normal to feel unsettled and as if you are losing your mind during deep and profound change (you are in a way—you're losing your conditioned mind); and it takes time to integrate and make habitual your new ways of being. Some of the deepest changes in me have taken years to become integrated as my new self. Feeling off-centre is a normal and expected part of the process.

You will know that progress is occurring in small ways. Your outside life might look like a car crash, but inside you'll feel shifts in awareness, more tolerance, more ability to reframe challenges as opportunities, less reactivity to old triggers, more mental spaciousness. You will 'fall off the wagon' sometimes and back into old destructive patterns and that's okay. That's normal. But you'll start to find it easier to let go of shaming and blaming yourself, and simply start over again tomorrow, no drama (in fact, having less drama in your life is a sure sign that you are living from the inside out more of the time). You may spend months 'off the wagon' but your intuition will prompt you back onto the path of your soul and you will be open to it, ready to follow it again. Your soul longs for expansion, spontaneity, exploration, and creativity. It wants to delight in life, to experience joy and love and the whole spectrum of what life has to offer. As the accumulated content of your layers and the programmes given to you by well-meaning others starts to clear, you will experience soft joy in everyday things, gentleness towards yourself, contentment with simplicity and slowness, and cease to take yourself so seriously.

My heartfelt desire is that you allow yourself to become full once more, just as you were the day you were born. May you accept and revel in the exquisite jigsaw piece that you are and find your way to the exact place where you truly fit, where you get to just be you and in doing so, add to the beauty of the whole picture; the place which allows the full radiance, the whole 100% of you, to shine forth rather than just the meagre 0.1%.

The world is in shadow right now. Popular culture and the cyber world are dark and hypnotic spaces which draw us trance-like into living even more from unconscious habit: simply getting by when we were born for so much more. In the past, we had only the programming of our childhood to scrutinise in order to grow. Nowadays you are being programmed all day, every day from what you give your attention to—through the toxic portal of your electronic devices. Algorithms act in the same way as the reticular activating system, bringing you more of what you give your attention to, repeatedly. The next time you are surfing social media pay attention to what you pause to look at and know you will be fed more of that.

If you watch hours of bad news, you'll be shown more bad news until you have a firm belief that the world is a terrible place, and you need to be vigilant and ready to defend yourself against it, ramping up the nervous system. What is that stance going to do to your relationships, your choices, and your sense of what you can achieve in the world?

Stop allowing people from the past and today's cyber algorithms to guide your thoughts, feelings, beliefs, and your life. Start living from the inside out by deciding what *you* want, what *you* love and who *you* want to be in this life. Give that your attention, clear away any old clutter that does not align with that vision, and let it start to flow outwards. It's time to stop letting the world tell you who you are, from the outside in, get into the driver's seat and start living on your terms: live from the inside out, in the pursuit of joy, and show the world just how magnificent you are.

"Tell me, what is it you plan to do
with your one wild and precious life?"

~Mary Oliver